NO COUNTY TO COMPARE

Memories of a Herefordshire Childhood
between the Wars

by

JOHN POLLARD

D1321876

LAPRIDGE PUBLICATIONS
1994

The author and publisher wish to thank
Hereford Library, Derek Foxton, and Weobley Museum
for permission to reproduce photographs

First published in 1994 by
Lapridge Publications
25 Church Street
Hereford HR1 2LR
© Copyright 1994 John Pollard

ISBN 0 9518589 5 5

Printed in Great Britain by
Redwood Books, Trowbridge, Wilts.

For my sisters Dorothy and Mary
and
Leonard Foster
who shared so much of this

Contents

A Note from the Author

'I will say that there's no county to compare with Herefordshire'
C. N. de Courcy-Parry

I caught what the famous huntsman de Courcy-Parry describes as the 'Hereford disease' very early in life and have suffered from it ever since. It is a kind of nostalgia which never leaves you and from which you never want to be cured. But then, anyone who lives there will tell you that Herefordshire is England at its best, which means in effect the world.

I arrived in the city of Hereford when barely a toddler, too young to heed talk of Zeppelin raids or an invisible presence called the war. My world was the Castle Green, strolls with my nanny along the Wye, out to Hampton Bishop or up Aylestone Hill. But most exciting of all was the annual May Fair; from the windows above Walmsley's, the big drapery emporium where Lloyds Bank now stands, I had a grandstand view. Alongside, the market clock chimed the hours while the cathedral in whose shadow I first went to school was only a short distance away. Visits to the station to see the steam engines or to Greenland's toy bazaar were varied by learning to fish in the river or excursions to the hills of Abergavenny and once to the sea at Porthcawl. It was the kind of life I would have been unwilling to change, though change came unexpectedly with a move to the country.

Weobley was country life writ large, with novelties like fields, ponds, birds and beasts, cider making and hop picking as well as sports. Learning to cope with the rigours of a village school was character-building if not all smooth going. But a new home brought a host of new acquaintances including a coachman straight out of Dickens, a sexton, a drover, a famous lady folklorist, farmers, farm workers and gentry, some affable, others eccentric, as well as lots of kindly women and friends among boys and girls. The workhouse, of all places, was a popular venue, where we were privileged to run wild and indulge all our whims. There we met the young Gilbert Harding of later television fame and his delightful rumbustious sister.

Country pursuits didn't end when I returned to Hereford to school, cycling daily to a station four miles distant from Weobley and all the way to the city during the general strike of 1926. Winning a rural scholarship was something new and didn't go down well with my erstwhile playmates who had left school at fourteen without the benefit of French or Algebra. But they still accompanied me on rambles round the lanes and fields, birds' nesting, chasing rabbits in the corn, fishing or toting a muzzle-loading gun. Then came disaster:

the business, like so many others in the late twenties, began to fail and finally had to be sold.

So the Hereford idyll ended, though not quite since we were not forgotten by old friends many of whom paid visits or wrote to keep us up to date with news. Many things intervened before I was privileged to visit Herefordshire again. One was World War II which took me to Africa and on to Oxford when it finally ended. Hereford had changed, but only superficially. The cathedral still dominated the western skyline, while the Wye rolled placidly on its way to join the Severn. Two world wars had revolutionised the lives of ordinary citizens, but less obviously those of the farming community: Weobley had the same olde worlde appearance as it had when I first saw it sixty years previously. Most delightful of all was to find the fair in Hereford's High Town very much in evidence during the first week in May, though the golden dragons had been long since superseded by more sophisticated creations. I was already beginning to sense a fresh onset of the Hereford malady as unwillingly I turned away.

John Pollard 1994

1. Golden Dragons

Something very odd was going on in the street below. A posse of roughly dressed men, with predatory features, was busy holding tape measures or scattering bits of wood for no readily explicable reason. Being Sunday the High Town was practically deserted, so they had the entire place to themselves. My brother and I, watching from the windows, were told they were preparing for the May Fair. But it wasn't until the following morning when the first of a series of showmen's engines edged round the corner that all the planning and measuring was explained.

The fair engines beat everything for sheer power and magnificence. They were traction engines with gleaming yellow driving wheels, higher than the tallest fairman, and dynamos perched crazily in front of their boilers. And all this snug beneath a broad white roof supported by twisted brasswork. The engines drew trailers laden with mechanical organs, dragon chariots and Edwardian motor-cars, roundabouts mounted on wheels and sets of galloping horses. We remained enthralled, noses pressed to the glass, while vast structures rose like fairy castles before our eyes. The dragons and motorcars were lifted by cranes, fitted to the traction engines, and lowered on to wooden rails. The scenic railways rose and fell about the electric organs, with their plastic angels, flitting cupids, drum-beating soldiers and dainty shepherdesses.

When evening came the lights on the roundabouts illuminated the city and suddenly everything came to life. The traction engines, parked unostentatiously against the kerbs to work the dynamos, pumped their pistons. Their chimneys seemed to reach the skies when fitted with the long extensions which took away the smoke. The red glow from the dragons' eyes, as they heaved and dived about the organs, the thunder of the motorcars and the reflected gleam from the revolving horses transformed the High Town into a wonderland whose marvels, when bedtime came, we were most reluctant to abandon.

Wednesday was market day and the streets were crowded with farmers and their families, all queuing to slide down the helter-skelter, ride on the horses, try their luck at hoop-la or venture, greatly daring, into Jacob Studt's giant poly-swing.

'Bend your knees, ladies! Bob up and down!' The portly fairman's vulgar injunctions were the source of much ribaldry as the sweating, red-faced hoydens did their best to comply.

Still the 'Welsh Golden Dragons' were the kings of the fair jungle. Their green serpentine heads with flaring nostrils and pricked fin ears seemed to rise and fall with the rhythm of the music. Even as they tossed and tumbled, a young showman, agile as a monkey, leaped and clung on to a gondola, collecting fares from the passengers holding on tightly in the red plush seats.

On Thursday afternoons the shops closed. This was the time when our father, relieved for a space from the cares of business, emerged with his small sons clinging to his hands. Although he possessed little skill as a thrower it was a point of honour with him never to return without a coconut, even though it cost him a pound. The shies were in Broad Street opposite the Green Dragon, the city's leading hotel. Its lively effigy above the entrance was intimately related in my childish view to the fabulous beasts of the fair.

The fair attained its apogée on Saturday night when the whole town went wild. Then it was unsafe for respectable folk to be abroad. Girls screamed in mingled fear and ecstasy as swains, rendered reckless by beer and cider, stuffed bags of confetti down mock-reluctant necks. A black pall of smoke hung over the city as the traction engines redoubled their efforts to keep the roundabouts and lights supplied. Sparks flashed from the dragons' wheels, drunks tripped over the electric cables, while the intoxicating strains of 'Where do flies go in the winter time?' reverberated on the spring air. Every now and then a fight broke out and policemen pushed through the packed throng. Then life was at its most raw, most rousing and most English as the crowds jostled and swayed round the sideshows and stalls in mutual abandon to garish pleasure. Our housemaids were there. So were the shop assistants, all decked out in cheap finery and sporting rakish tams. It was the happiest time of their normally drab lives and they were determined to make the most of it.

But the fair didn't last. Like Halley's comet it blazed briefly, only to fade away. By the following Sunday morning it was all pulled down and the Salvation Army band resumed its rightful place. Sadly, oh so sadly we watched it depart, cheered only by the reflection that it was as sure to return the following year as the merry month itself.

When the fair had gone the High Town did not lack for music since an itinerant harpist played outside the shops. A skilled performer, the loud thrum of the strings on the big golden instrument, from which he coaxed lively and familiar airs, gave cheer to the passers-by as Apollo did for the Olympians. The shopkeepers paid him, for they found it worth their while to encourage people to pause and admire the goods on sale.

We lived above the shop and enjoyed an eagle's eye view of everything that went on in the street below. Walmsleys, the big drapery emporium in the centre of the High Town, stood near the market clock. It was one of the most imposing edifices in the city, with a facade of pilasters worthy of a Graeco-Roman temple. My father, à la House of Elliot, employed a bevy of shopgirls of varying age and charm, all staidly dressed in long black costumes. There

2

Walmsley's Cash Drapers, High Town. Now the site of Lloyds Bank.

were also two maids and an odd-job boy called Bert, who performed heavier tasks, like bringing in the bags of anthracite to feed the stoves which heated the shop. We were fond of Bert, a tall intelligent lad, willing to turn his hand to anything.

In addition to my mother who, like my father, had been trained in business, her maiden aunt Rose, known as Nana, came to live with us. She brought with her Emmie, the orphan daughter of a family friend, who both served in the shop and assisted Nana and whom we all came to love. Nana's rôle was twofold. First and foremost she took charge of the children and secondly she ran the kitchen. She was a splendid cook and my mother relied upon her to organise the domestic affairs, which she did most efficiently. Nana was of average height, slim and in her youth good-looking. She had a cheerful, attractive face and bright red cheeks, but could be as fierce as a tigress in defence of us children. Like so many Victorian women she had been dissuaded from marrying because her family disapproved of her suitor. But her spinster-hood was our gain and we all owed an incalculable debt to Nana. Nana never travelled far except once for a weekend with her sister in Paris. They visited the Louvre, but it was the 'little dark Frenchmen' she remembered best.

I was born in Exeter, but when my father secured a post with the wholesale drapery firm of Baker Baker we moved to Bristol where he was fated to meet Herbert Mills. Mills's mother had recently inherited Walmsley's, and her husband, a retired bank inspector, was looking for someone to manage the business. This wasn't easy in 1915, but since my father appeared to be hard working and honest it was decided to give him a trial.

Herbert Mills was of medium height and I suppose about thirty, with thin features, like his father's, which could light up in a bright smile when anything amused him. He also spoke with a public school accent, as befitted an old Cliftonian. He was a friendless soul and when a land girl, whom my father had befriended, moved out of one of the two attics Herbert duly moved in. The land girl had had an illegitimate child, not an uncommon occurrence during the war, but this was sufficient to debar her from employment in the eyes of the godly. Pitying her plight my father had employed her as a tailor and seamstress.

Herbert was a fringe intellectual and a devotee of occult science. A firm believer in the teachings of Madame Blavatsky and Annie Besant and other leading lights of the Theosophical school, he would retire for hours to commune with Indian and Tibetan adepts whom he claimed to encounter on an astral plane. When engaged in such communion he would fast for days and, on the rare occasions when he rejoined the family he would remain stolidly silent like a man in a trance.

For a time he retired to a cottage in a remote hamlet called Westhope, where he adopted the style of living of a mediaeval anchorite. We visited him there once, but all I recall was the blazing wood fire. But he soon tired of his own company and returned to Walmsley's carrying a long black case. It contained a brass telescope which he would poke through the attic skylight and gaze at the moon. Tiring of astronomy he took to the road and ended his life in an asylum.

Herbert was kind to Tommy and me and sometimes took us for walks. The one I remember was, predictably enough, to Belmont Abbey, where Tommy amused him by seating himself comfortably in a chair-like kneeler. The visit was during the autumn, because when we came out boys were busy knocking conkers from the chestnut trees. On the way home I saw an otter swimming in the Bishop's Pool.

My father was not only good at figures but also a fine musician. The dining room at Walmsley's housed my mother's piano on which he would perform. His favourite was the 'Entry of the Gladiators', but his repertoire included many of the best known Victorian favourites like 'Because', 'The Holy City', 'A Jovial Monk', the Toreador's song from *Carmen* and 'I'll sing thee songs of Araby', all of which he knew by heart and would accompany in his fine baritone voice. He also played the violin. So I was brought up to appreciate music, since my mother also played and sang.

My father was highly intelligent and surprisingly well read. Dickens was his favourite author and he read him all his life. He also liked the thrillers of Guy Boothby and Sax Rohmer, both best-sellers in their day. But he couldn't stand detail and avoided women novelists.

My mother, on the other hand, was a practical woman, who kept my father on the rails. This wasn't always easy, but in the end she usually got her way. He always deferred to her in a crisis and life for him was filled with many. Managing a large business was a new experience, but with my mother there to support him my father gained in confidence and began to do well. Rejected for the army, though he had once served in the Devon Volunteers, he became a special constable.

While staying in lodgings prior to moving into Walmsley's I celebrated my first birthday and received a card from my mother's eldest sister. It was a tinted photo of the gorgeous Gladys Cooper which I still treasure.

I fear I must disagree with Sir Fred Hoyle who maintains, in his entertaining autobiography, that nobody recalls events prior to their fifth birthday, since I have a clear recollection of being carried by my father round Walmsley's when I was fifteen months old. Again I well remember February 22 1916, the day my brother was born. Pain too is memorable. Between the ages of one and two I fell out of the back of a horse brake when my father failed to clutch me after opening the rear door. Then, a little later, I slipped on the ice.

The winter of 1916–1917 was a severe one, as troops in the trenches could have told you. For the first time in memory the Wye froze over and my parents, with my mother pushing my infant brother in the pram, decided to join the crowd disporting beside the old Wye bridge. It was a dangerous spot, for against the further bank the current flowed black and evil. Inevitably I fell, not once, but several times, learning the hard way that ice is not walkable.

During the summer I learned also that bees sting, when I was attacked while seated among some flowers on a railway trolley at the station.

More memorable was visiting Hancock's fair in the cattle market. I can still see, in my mind's eye, old Hancock with his peg leg standing beside a shy filled with crockery and being invited to 'break a cup'. My mother protested at such vandalism in wartime, but despite my childish efforts the cups remained intact.

Then there was the dancing bear. It arrived one day across the street in charge of a man I was told was a gypsy. It had a ring in its nose attached to a length of rope, but I was far too young to appreciate the cruelty.

'Yah, yah yah!' the gypsy chanted, savagely jerking the lead. So encouraged the bear rose clumsily to its feet and rocked from side to side. Such spectacles are still common in eastern Europe, though long since banned in the west. Yet bear baiting a century or two ago was a favourite sport in England, when the wretched beasts were worried to death.

Long before I could read or write I used to copy the name on the shops opposite. Of these BOOTS THE CASH CHEMISTS, MAYPOLE DAIRY and GREENLANDS were the most eye-catching. Of course I didn't know what the names signified, or that I was growing up in a world dominated by shops and traders. Nana sometimes took me shopping, which I enjoyed. Shops, I decided, were nice places stocked with things to eat like chocolates, or things to buy like toys. But Nana, for some reason, seemed deliberately to avoid sweet shops and toy shops in favour of bakers and grocers. Still, it was all very exciting being trailed around and introduced to friendly shopkeepers, even though you had nothing to say. One day my brother, who was all of two, dragged away a wooden horse, which was standing outside Turner's toy-shop. Nana failed at first to notice and it was only when we were almost home that she discovered the innocent felony. So there was nothing for it but to return to the shop and explain what had happened. But her cheeks rather burned.

I have mentioned that we employed maids, which nowadays might suggest we were rich, whereas at the time it was the norm. That is not to say that everyone employed unmarried girls, but if you required them you could usually afford to do so. It was hard for girls to obtain employment outside domestic service and it suited many to find a post with a local family, so enabling them to live at home. An elder girl liked to bring a sister, who had just left school, and could assist with the chores. So Edith brought Amy and under the benevolent rule of Nana my mother was free to attend to business. Edith, if memory serves, wore a white apron and a matching cap, whereas Amy was dressed in her workaday clothes. For payment they received only a few shillings a week, but that was sufficient to live on. When they got married girls abandoned service for good and were supported by their husbands' wages. In effect young women often married in order to give up work and devote their life to their homes and children, a far cry from life today when expectations are considerably higher. Maids in those days rarely or never went on holiday, except with the family, and were content, like most people, with the amenities provided by the place they lived in. Girls living in a delightful rural setting like Herefordshire were, of course, favoured, unlike those who were confined to large towns. There was no social security, at least on the modern scale.

We also employed a washerwoman, named Mrs Richards, who came round once a week. So the maids' tasks were limited and they were far from overworked, leaving time, if they were willing, to take a hand with the children. They naturally varied in quality. Nellie used to sit with her elbows on the table and corrected me severely when I called rabbits 'bunnies'. But she was an exception. Edith was neat and clean, but had little time for children. Maids could be and doubtless were an advantage. On the other hand, since they shared your life, they always knew what was going on.

2 World War I, Porthcawl and Abergavenny

Hereford was not a place you would associate with war, yet during 'fourteen-eighteen', as the soldiers termed it, it not only suffered a kind of trauma from the threat of air raids but also played a valuable rôle in supplying munitions to the troops at the front. The munition works were sited out of the city at Rotherwas, where hundreds of girls were employed. They didn't all come from Hereford but arrived in batches from other places. Most were peacefully inclined, but there were elements ready to beat up the town which they sometimes did on Saturday nights after drinking in the local pubs. Worse was when the sirens sounded from the electric light works, warning everyone to take cover since Zeppelins were about. In such circumstances the girls working in the munition factory were clearly most vulnerable and when the warning came at night time, as it usually did, they would come screeching through the streets like a flock of frightened canaries, their complexions as yellow as the cordite which was their stock in trade. I was always abed when this happened, but Nana's and Emmie's descriptions were graphic indeed.

What I did see were soldiers in light blue uniforms wandering round the High Town on crutches. When I inquired who they were I was told 'wounded soldiers', for Hereford was a reception centre for the maimed. For some reason I christened them 'wounded bonbons' and for years the name stuck. When later anyone mentioned the war, the subject of wounded bonbons invariably came up. I was merely intrigued by the sight of these legless or armless men, puffing pipes and cigarettes, as they stopped to talk to strangers or trudged listlessly about. Of the horrors to which they had been subjected I knew nothing, though I was alarmed by references to the war, about which everyone was talking. The word, in my childish ears, sounded onomatopoeic and terrifying, rendered worse by its patent invisibility. What was this war, I wondered, which made even Nana and my mother look grave, and what were Zeppelins? As the war went on I learned from the grownups that when Zeppelins came you ran down to the cellar. Since the cellar at Walmsley's was dark, dank and highly insalubrious Zeppelins which drove you there were clearly something awful. They never arrived, but the threat of their coming was constantly there. What was even more frightening was the occasional growl of aircraft overhead. It made me want to run away and hide, when everyone else leaned out of the windows in order to obtain a better view. The point was that they flew overhead and it was from the skies that air raids came. But when my mother took me to watch an air show at Aberga-venny my attention was soon diverted to a stall selling replica toy planes. They were made of aluminium, out of spare material used in the manufacture of real planes. In the end my mother was persuaded to buy one, a biplane with red, white and blue discs on the wings. I kept it for years and only wish I had it now, to put on display at the Antiques Road Show. In those days nobody realised the potential future value of toys, or indeed of genuine antiques. I once, while a boy, bought a brace of old pistols for half a crown in an antique shop in Church Street and the old man in charge was so delighted that he threw in a loader and powder flask too. But then, sixty-five years ago few people had money to waste on articles they didn't need.

In the meantime people were queuing at ten shillings and six pence a time to enjoy the thrill of flying. One flapper, as young women were known in the early twenties, told my mother excitedly that she had just 'looped the loop'. What looping the loop meant I hadn't the faintest notion, but I could tell from my mother's face that she too would have liked to risk a flight, had she been able to afford the fee.

Farmers, as a class, appeared to ignore the war, since they weren't directly involved. They were primarily food providers and did very well with the help of subsidies, until these were withdrawn in 1921.

'At any rate they've got nice weather for it,' a farmer's wife said one day in the shop.

'That's all they thought of it!' Emmie observed later in disgust. But then there was no reason why farmers should have been especially concerned about a conflict of which they knew nothing. At that time the media as we know it didn't exist. There was no wireless or television. Only the papers spread news. But farmers had no time to read, much less to discuss events unconnected with farming. Farmers were busy men, few indeed more so. They did their job, ploughing and getting in the harvest, breeding cattle and sheep or engaging in milk production. Few possessed tractors and the farm economy was largely horse-based. So horses had to be looked after too and fed like the other stock. Farmers' wives had to feed their menfolk and supply hens, eggs and butter in their spare time. This is not to pretend that many farmers' sons didn't serve in the trenches. Many did and died, together with farm labourers. But the majority were busy growing food and exempted from military service. So one shouldn't be too hard on the wife in the shop, who was probably making a joke anyhow.

As for Zeppelins, I don't recall taking refuge in the cellar, though I have some recollection of being woken at night, wrapped in a blanket and carried downstairs. Probably the siren announcing that the threat of a raid was over sounded in time. It was, at any rate, an alarming experience for anyone, and in particular a child, to be roused from sleep. Worse was the realisation that the grownups were helpless and didn't know what to do. Till then they had proved reliable, but suddenly dependability had disappeared with the war. At times rather to their surprise I burst into tears of incomprehension when I heard my parents discussing some new horror. The fact is that children, and even young children, understand far more than they are given credit for and I was no exception.

People directly involved in the war sometimes called, like my mother's brother George, who died of pneumonia, and her handsome half-brother Ernest. Ernest, who ended the war as a brigade major, had proved such a good instructor that he had been kept at home training troops. But he was released for the final push in 1918 and charged through the enemy lines in his tank. His driver was killed, but he survived to become an officer, responsible for movement, first on the London and North Western and, after it amalgamated, with the London, Midland and Scottish Railway. I still possess a card which he sent from the front. For security reasons you were allowed to write virtually nothing. The card is dated January 6 1918 and has the answers already printed. It was misaddressed to my mother at 'High Street, Hereford', instead of High Town, but was safely delivered. At the top is a warning 'Nothing is to be written on this side except the date and signature of the sender. If anything else is added the post card will be destroyed'.

Below, Ernest underlined in pencil the printed information 'I am quite well'. The rest, like 'I have been admitted into hospital' or 'I am being sent down to the base', is crossed out. Such was news from the trenches in bare outline. Yet even that was welcome in a war in which casualties were counted in thousands and in which it was hard to survive. There was, in addition, the pointlessness of it all, as though it had been arranged to please the generals. The men who fought went like game before the guns, because there was no escape. Cowardice was punished by a firing squad, so you preferred to go over the top with the others, hoping for a blighty one, or at least a quick death. There was one pathetic sentence on the card which I have omitted. The longing for news from home, a line from a loved one, a touch of normality amid all the slaughter. 'I have received no letter from you for a long time'. Now that war is forgotten, having been succeeded by another, except by those involved in it, even in a humble way. To me The War is still World War I even though I served in the other.

German prisoners of war were incarcerated all over the country, including quiet regions like Herefordshire. Most of them were thankful to be out of the line, safe and well fed in Britain. Many worked on farms and were willing to do so since farms were the source of food. One day I saw two prisoners for myself. As a small boy one of my favourite walks with my mother was down to the

Barr's Court Station, Hereford.

station to see the engines. Hereford station, like many others, was built deliberately far from the town centre. Nobody welcomed the fumes and smoke, a necessary concomitant of steam locomotives, or the noise made by trains arriving in the night. As it was a good mile from High Town failure to hire a cab or other conveyance involved a long walk, often carrying heavy baggage. But the Victorians who planned the railways were not concerned with this: in their day, everyone except the rich normally travelled on foot.

After admiring my two favourite engines *County Clare* and *Jackdaw* I happened to notice two soldiers, wearing forage caps, standing against the barrier. The colour of their uniforms was unfamiliar, being, instead of the familiar khaki, field grey. When my mother explained that they were German prisoners of war I was mystified. I had heard much about Germans over the past years and had always imagined that they were some kind of monster. To my surprise the men looked perfectly ordinary, like Englishmen in fact. In addition they appeared very mild and peaceful, not warlike or fierce at all. The younger, who was clean shaven, smiled at me, or perhaps at my mother, while the other who was older and wore a moustache seemed to gaze through us into space. Probably he was wondering what was going on at home and whether his family had enough to eat. Or perhaps his sensibilities had been dulled by his experiences and he no longer expected much of fate. At any rate the pair have remained in my memory when other things have faded. Even now I can see them standing there, while I watched them with wondering eyes.

As for the 'wounded bonbons', they gradually left the High Town and the adjoining streets. Many, after leaving hospital, had been domiciled in the mansions of the gentry prior to being sent home. Presumably this happened to the 'bonbons' too.

One day, when I was very young, my mother decided to walk to Credenhill. Credenhill is a good five miles from Hereford, but she thought little of that. In those days everyone walked everywhere, since virtually nobody possessed a car. My mother had been brought up at Abergavenny and was used to walking the hills. The reason for the outing was a country fête, presumably in aid of the war. Of course walking on a main road was not the hazard it is today as traffic was a rarity and easy to avoid, since you could always hear it coming.

As it was a hot summer day my mother brought the pram in case I got tired, leaving my baby brother at home with Nana. She brought a kettle to make tea in case we became thirsty, and asked a woman in a cottage to fill it with hot water. The woman obliged and after quenching our thirst we proceeded.

Credenhill, like Dinedor, overlooking Hereford, is the site of an iron age camp, but we didn't know that and were only concerned with finding the whereabouts of the fête. To the best of my recollection it took place in a park, or the garden of a country house on the village outskirts. We appear to have arrived in time for tea, for I remember little else. We sat on the grass and were plagued with flies, while sandwiches were handed round in a basket. I was given what I took for one spread with raspberry jam, only to discover, to my horror, it was tomato. There is nothing especially horrible about tomato sandwiches, indeed they form the staple of most picnics, only I had never encountered tomatoes before and have tended to avoid them since. On the return journey I believe I took to the pram, while my mother completed the ten mile hike.

Holidays were possible during the war and we visited Porthcawl, a favourite and accessible seaside place. My mother's sister Dora had come to stay, with her small son and infant daughter, while her husband was serving in the East African campaign against General von Lettow-Vorbeck. Having been repeatedly assured that she had nothing to fear from the air raids, the sirens sounded the night we left and she duly made her way to the cellar. One glance at the Stygian interior was enough to persuade her rather to face doom in the shop, with her daughter propped on the counter.

As we crossed the Wye by the railway bridge a large bird rose. 'Expect it's a wild duck,' Nana observed to Emmie, though I suspect it was a heron.

12

Porthcawl was and is as popular with South Walians and border people as Blackpool with Lancastrians, but it is much smaller and altogether more pukka, with a fine golf course and hotel where the rugby Barbarians are accommodated. It has two bays: Rest Bay, which is rocky and where we pricked our feet, and Sandy Bay which speaks for itself. What I remember best were the bathing machines, mobile changing huts, popular in Victorian times. They had four wheels and were drawn by horses into the surf at high tide. Changing on the beach was not allowed, while the sexes were segregated. Men and women emerged from the machines wearing long black costumes designed to disguise the figure. Some women wore skirts over their costumes or even hoops and extravagant headgear. Since few could swim, bathing consisted for the most part of bobbing up and down in the water.

Tommy and I wore highly uncomfortable waders made out of stiff material. The elastic left weals on our legs and we were relieved to abandon them in the evening. I was reminded of the war when a four funnelled battleship sailed across the horizon.

Nana's Cheltonian brother and sister were invited to join us, together with their respective spouses. Jolly obese uncle Walter threw pebbles into a pool to amuse us, pretending the splashes were caused by fish, and also flew a kite. When he ventured into the sea and floated everyone was loud in his praise. But then nobody else could swim.

I didn't visit Porthcawl again for sixty years. It had hardly changed at all.

The war ended on November 11 1918 and everyone looked forward to the first peaceful Christmas for four years. To celebrate the family gathered at my mother's elder sister's house in Abergavenny. Abergavenny in the Usk valley is a delectable place, where I was destined to spend my holidays. It lay twenty four miles south-west of Hereford and was known as the 'Gate of Wales'. We travelled by train and I remember the stops, all of which have since disappeared. Tram Inn was the first, followed by St Devereux, Pontrilas, Pandy and Abergavenny Junction. Few used the main Great Western station which, like Hereford's, lay too far out of town. At the Junction you not only changed trains, but railways as well. I was intrigued by the novelty of the cream and chocolate coaches of the London and North Western Railway, the finely sewn old gold upholstery, and the thundering black locos.

My aunt's house was built of red brick, half hidden by a Virginia creeper. It was sited half way up the Brest with a view over the Usk to the Blorenge. It was called 'Lewes', the Marquis of Abergavenny's second title, since it had been built on his land. My mother remembered this friend of King Edward, 'a big man with a sandy moustache', who drove up in a buggy to inspect the building.

On Boxing Day everyone assembled in the Blue Room, the room which was reserved for special occasions. Whether it was my mother's or Emmie's idea to wrap all the presents in cardboard shells is academic. At all events the effect was dramatic. The shells were ranged in rows with the biggest for the menfolk at the back. My mother, amid laughter, advised recipients to handle the missiles with care and on no account to drop them, for fear they might explode.

Later my father produced a toy cardboard stage on which he made puppets dance, manoeuvring them from the rear. As each took a bow he pretended it was one of the children present, while my uncle provided music on a mouth organ. My uncle had played rugby for Newport and Wales, and was a cricketer of note. But you would never have guessed it since his manners were so perfect that some found them embarrassing. He was also tall and very good looking, with one grey eye and one blue. He pronounced Abergavenny as 'Abergenny', like the Marquis's title.

There was never another Christmas like the Christmas at Lewes, but then the circumstances were unique.

So the Great War had ended and everyone wondered what the future would bring. The High Town turned back to normal, though there were changes like an increase in traffic, not to mention clothes. Men out of khaki paraded in suits, trilbies and spats, while ladies wore long filmy dresses and strings of beads as well as broad hats. As for music, ragtime had become popular during the war and everyone was 'doing it', even in public. There was a new sense of freedom. Former inhibitions were cast aside and the 'cake walk' ousted the Lancers at the local dance. Women, emancipated by service in the war, now demanded the vote and eventually got it, while others joined the professions.

The following Christmas the same Cheltenham elders who had stayed with us at Porthcawl arrived to share the celebrations. My own contribution was to distribute presents disguised as Father Christmas. Proud of my knowledge of locomotives I drew for great uncle Walter's benefit a picture of *County Clare*. To my great annoyance he sketched in a dome, the one feature which Great Western engines, for the most part, lack. In order to prove my point I dragged him off to the station and indicated several domeless examples.

'But they ought to have, didn't they?' he defended weakly, so anticipating the Reverend Awdry's view that domeless engines were hardly respectable.

Better than Father Christmas was the sale. My father was anxious to get rid of prewar stock and shirts were being offered at a penny each, while other garments were marked down in proportion. By opening time an enormous queue stretched all down the High Town, and when the joking suggestion was made that the ladies from Cheltenham might care to assist the shopgirls they eagerly agreed and had the time of their normally staid lives.

14

3 Shops and Traffic

The aftermath of the war saw a boom in trade from which my father benefitted. Despite the enormous casualties unemployment was rife, at least in the larger towns. However an agriculturally based economy like Herefordshire's didn't suffer so much and in some ways hardly at all. To begin with there were no big factories once the munition girls had left. Wages were still low so that shopkeepers could hire assistants at very little cost.

The renamed Bon Marché did well on a rising market and my parents were engaged in frequent visits to the wholesalers in Bristol. The extent of their purchases alarmed Mills senior, until his accountant lent his backing to their enterprise. Deciding that the property required modernising my father engaged a builder, named Bailey, to construct an arcade window as well as a private side entrance. He met the consequent increase in rates by letting a portion of the shop to Curry's, the cycle firm. Accommodation was provided for the manager, his wife and small son adjacent to our own and we became quite friendly. Weston was a blond Midlander who, unlike my father, knew about machines. On the other hand my father knew about books and found the next-door shop of Jakeman & Carver irresistible. As a result I am still the possessor of Cassell's *History of England* and *Railway Wonders of the World*, as well as other volumes. Jakeman & Carver's was a happy hunting ground for parsons and it was there that my father met the vicar of Kilpeck. At the latter's invitation we took the train to St Devereux and walked the half mile to the church. We came to view the door and other Norman antiquities which, as a small boy, left me cold. As a general rule we didn't go to church, though Nana and Emmie attended All Saints. My father was put off by the high-church ceremony there at Christmas when the priest rang a bell, shook clouds of incense from a censer and led round a donkey for good measure.

Occasionally the clergy patronised the shop. One parson was in the habit of purchasing goods for some charitable institution and delaying payment for a year. When he finally did settle his account he immediately placed an order for another lot of goods. Thus, in effect, he lived on credit. My father determined to put an end to this practice, which had started under his predecessor. So, after supplying the goods he sent out a bill. The result was electric. The bill had had scarcely time to arrive when the angry parson appeared in the shop.

'What's the fellow's name?' he demanded rudely, quizzing the offending document at arm's length.

The 'fellow' in question duly closed the account and the parson was obliged to take his custom elsewhere.

Jakeman & Carver, printers and booksellers, High Town.

During the twenties the clergy were badly paid and many of them were obliged to take advantage of their position and live, for the most part, on their wits. This did not, of course, apply to the higher clergy, like deans, archdeacons, bishops and such. Cathedrals varied considerably in their endowment and the stipend of the bishop of Hereford was four thousand a year, a considerable fortune at the time. Most were around two thousand, apart from Durham, where the bishop enjoyed the princely fortune of fifteen thousand, which put him on a par with peers and tycoons.

Later the stipends were evened out, doubtless much to the chagrin of such prelates as were better endowed. But the activities of bishops and high church dignitaries were a closed book to us. They had no social contact with tradesmen, or tradesmen with them.

There were many interesting shops in the High Town and its environs during the period, most of which I got to know well. The day of the big stores was yet to come, but Woolworths and Marks & Spencer soon moved in. Immediately after the war it was still the day of the family business, when everyone tended to know everyone else. Younger children attended the same school as we did, while my parents were on friendly terms with many of the shopkeepers in the district.

The market hall was a prominent feature in the High Town, crowned as it was with the clock. The clock peeped over the roof above the attics, looking like Big Ben, so we always knew the time whether at home or in the street. The lady who ran the market, Mrs Tranter, supplied us with vegetables and fruit. Shortly after we left Hereford the market caught fire and provided one of the most awesome spectacles that the city had ever seen. Had we still been in residence the effect of a major fire next door would have been appalling, and could have involved vacating the premises in the middle of the night. Fires at the shops were quite common at the time and I once slept through a conflagration at the draper's shop opposite.

Gurney's, the leading grocers, held a special fascination for me. Money taken at the counter was screwed up in a metal container and despatched along a wire by a pull on a string to a cashier seated in a cubicle. She in turn unscrewed the canister, checked the chit sent with the money, and returned the change by the same aerial route.

Lower down in Commercial Street was the Slatter's grocery shop. Mr and Mrs Slatter confronted you together from behind the counter with greetings and welcoming smiles. They were generally regarded as the best looking couple in the city and their good looks were passed on to their children, Doris, Monica, Roy and Norman, who became a lieutenant-colonel in World War II.

From my view-point in High Town I could see, starting from the left, the

'Old House', the last black and white building in the city centre, which, at the time, was occupied by Lloyds Bank. Opposite was Gus Edwards, the 'Furrier of the West'. His shop held a special attraction for a boy familiar with such tales as Red Ridinghood, as a stuffed wolf grinned like Grandma from the window. Next came Oliver, the boot and shoe maker, Duck, Son & Pinker, the pianoforte dealers, Stead & Simpson also of shoe fame, the Domestic Bazaar, and Maypole Dairy, a big clean shop which smelt of cheese and butter; then Frank Stewart, the watchmaker, George Mason, yet another sizeable grocer, the King's Acre Florists (the King's Acre Nurseries lay a mile or two outside the city), Cope's, the site of the fire, later Wakefield Knight, the draper, Boots the chemists and finally the house of Greenland. Greenland's were furnishers, but to a child more famous for their Christmas toy fair. It was most exciting to hurry through the furniture and upholstery departments before entering a veritable wonderland. Toys of every kind and make fairly made your mouth water. If you wanted a present there and then you paid a shilling and an electric train would arrive with a wrapped parcel. Opening it was exciting, though it usually turned out to be something you didn't want. But then what could you expect for a shilling?

Below Greenlands, just out of sight, was the 'Penny Bazaar', shortly to become Marks & Spencer. As for the shops on the same side as Walmsley's, Bell's tobacconist's stood on the corner of Widemarsh Street, next to the cake shop run by the two Miss Matthews, pleasant young women with fashionable hairdos who always wore smiles. Ralph and Clarke, the chemist, stood alongside Russell, the stationer. I well remember Mr Ralph – or was it Mr Clarke? – a big man with a handsome open face and brisk efficient manner. At Russell's I bought the 'Rainbow', with its stories of Mrs Bruin and her boys, and later the 'Zoo Pictorial' that stimulated an early interest in animals and birds which has remained with me throughout my life. Then came Norman May, the photographer, Morton's shoes and finally Curry's. The manager, Weston, employed a friendly assistant, named Miss Richards, who dressed and talked like a man and was in a permanent good humour. She knew a lot about engines and cycles and such and let us try out the pedal cars in the shop.

'You'll never make a motor-man,' she would grin, as I knocked down a stand laden with batteries and bulbs. The fact was that I coveted a pedal motor more than anything else in life. But I never got one. My brother was luckier and received a tricycle for his birthday.

In St Owen's Street was the butcher's shop kept by Will and Albert Jonathan. They were related to my mother, since her eldest sister had married their eldest brother. All butchers are reputed to be jolly and Albert, in particular, was no exception. He was as round as a ball and, like all his brothers,

High Town in the 1920s.

an expert at games. He excelled at golf and billiards and made an annual pilgrimage to Twickenham to watch the Oxford versus Cambridge rugby match. As a butcher he prospered, owned a car and bought his wife, who didn't drive, a pony and trap.

I was once invited to accompany her and her daughter to Mordiford, only to find the Wye in flood and blocking the road. To find a road impassable was a new experience and I was relieved when we turned round and made for home. The daughter Nancy was very pretty. I found her presence embarrassing and was at a loss as how to deal with her teasing. Her father, who affected a semi-refined accent, called her 'Nence', and was delighted when she later excelled at tennis. Her mother dressed her up as a fairy and, from an early age, she appeared in public dancing displays. To my secret annoyance even my father would flirt with her whenever she called at the house. Nana too always treated her with deference and during her visits I found myself ignored.

Carnivals took place at stated intervals, when shopkeepers hired lorries and drays to advertise their wares. Scouts with their bugle band joined in as well as representatives of the corporation. The sweet sellers tossed samples among the crowds, which scrambled eagerly to get them. Some were thrown high right up to the windows, but I was never lucky. Jones' was the best known sweet shop in Hereford, situated in lower Church Street. It was still there when I visited the city some years ago, under new management, but with the old name still inscribed on the mat space below the door. Nobody in those days ever said that sweets were bad for the teeth.

Flags were in vogue and my father displayed big union jacks, made of bunting, on most festive occasions from the end of the war.

Cinemas provided entertainment during the evenings and also on Thursday afternoons. The Garrick in Widemarsh Street was probably the best known, but my father, who disliked going out at night, preferred matinée performances in the 'Kinema' off Broad Street. There we would watch Charlie Chaplin comedies heralded by advertisements, including that of the Bon Marché, projected on slides.

On one occasion a wild west circus visited the city. I was captivated by the posters depicting hordes of Indians attacking a stagecoach, only to find, when we attended a performance, that it was all on a far smaller scale.

The Three Counties Show was a novel experience for boys bred in town. The bulls impressed us most with their nose-rings and rolling eyes, though it was hard to believe in their vaunted ferocity. Mostly they lay panting in the summer heat, along with fat pigs and unshorn sheep. The cattle were almost all whitefaced Herefords, with occasional shorthorns and Ayrshire cows. Friesians and Charolais hadn't yet been heard of.

It is difficult these days to realise how light traffic was in the early nineteen twenties, so light in the High Town that I used to amuse my mother and Nana, watching from a window, when I ran across the street dodging vehicles. As I was holding my brother's hand such conduct appears doubly culpable, except that traffic was regarded as comparatively harmless because there were so little about.

Once a week a lordly carriage and pair would draw up outside. It contained two elderly ladies, with a coachman on the box. The coachman wore a grey, military style moustache, turned up at the ends, while his face was as red as the sinking sun on a cold November evening. Probably he possessed what is known as an 'expensive complexion', but I was too young to know that. He would get down from the box to hold the door open for the ladies, who would then proceed in stately fashion towards the nearest shops. At the other end of the social scale were occasional waggoners lashing cart horses, with the poor brutes' knees all but scraping the tarmac as they strove to drag trees weighing several tons. Such scenes drove Nana wild, as she was specially fond of horses. On market days cattle sometimes strayed into the High Town to be chased out by drovers yelling colourful oaths.

Motor cars with tilted backs and big brass headlamps sometimes passed by. So did Foden steam lorries, motorbikes and scooters. The postwar era was notable for an increase in types of mechanical vehicles, though few could yet afford a car. None but doctors, the rich and my uncle Albert possessed a vehicle, though some bakers owned a van. Across the road the rows of hansom cabs were being replaced slowly by taxis to take passengers to the station. But all these were as nothing where the ladies were concerned.

Every other morning the fashionable Miss Workman, whose family kept an ironmongers in Commercial Street, paraded like a gaudy butterfly up and down the street. Then my mother and Nana would run to the nearest window, while the shopgirls left their counters and crowded forward to see. So the High Town kept lively except on Sundays and Thursday afternoon. Then business ceased and few stirred abroad apart from church-goers. During Sunday evenings the Salvation Army band marched into the High Town and stationed itself opposite. My brother and I loved it, and did our best to imitate the music and reproduce the big drum's thump on our toy instruments. So life was jolly where two small boys were concerned, since there was always plenty to divert them. In addition to people, traffic and shops there was always a host of kindly females in attendance.

In those days the classes kept rigidly separate. It wasn't so much that they refused to mix as they simply didn't want to. Much the same obtains today, except that the division is less obvious. As for professional people like lawyers and accountants, as far as most tradesmen were concerned they didn't exist socially, for a man of professional status ran the risk of losing caste if he began to hobnob with people of lesser standing. The only time they came into contact was on a business level when a shop closed down or its owner had got into debt. I never recall meeting any but tradesmen's children during our seven year sojourn in Hereford. The only members of the professional classes we encountered were family doctors, who came to advise when we caught childish ailments or during my mother's accouchements. I remember them both, doctors Butler and Tullis.

Butler was older and wore a dark suit, and in general had little to say. Tullis, on the other hand, was young and rumbustious after service, I think, in the army. Both came to operate at the house when I suffered from adenoids. I recall little of this except when the chloroform mask was placed over my face one of them, probably Tullis, said 'If you don't like it, blow it away!' The operation was successful and I didn't meet either physician again until my brother and I contracted measles. Measles isn't usually serious and we soon became bored with staying in bed. Indeed we made such a rumpus that Tullis, who had called to see how we were getting on, arrived in the bedroom waving a dog-whip. The whip belonged to our smooth-haired fox-terrier Jack, who proved to be a champion ratter. It had soon been discovered that Walmsley's was overrun with rats, which my father trapped in cages. The problem was what to do next? Drown them? This we sometimes did, watching their feeble struggles till they turned on their backs. Or course them? Jack proved to be the answer. My father would release the rats from the cage in an empty room and set Jack to chase them.

4 Castle Green, Dinedor and Hampton Bishop

We had no garden, and the Castle Green provided us with a worthy substitute. The great thing was it was so near. We simply had to cross the High Town, turn up Church Street into the Close, pass by the Cathedral and through the iron gates, turn right by the Cathedral School into Quay Street and there you were. There we ran up and down the grassy banks, which hid the ruins of the ancient walls, or rode our scooters along the tarmac paths. There on the sward Nana would park the pram while we engaged in a game of bat and ball. The old cannon, known as Roaring Meg, a relic of the Crimean War, pointed threateningly down river. I never learned how it was acquired, or the history of the others guarding the column in the centre. We liked to climb up the steps, cut into the wooden gun-carriage, and sit boldly astride it as if it had been an iron horse. It was moved some years ago to Churchill Gardens.

One spot was sacred and that was the bowling green, kept immaculate by the groundsman Mr Dawson who, like his kind, forbade any violation of the hallowed square. On the approaches to the Green there were gardens too, neatly hedged with box. A friend, Roy Willetts, lived in a villa nearby and another, Keith Sinclair, in a house below. Roy and I eventually attended the High School. Keith came to my dame school and was usually to be found playing on the Green. He had beautiful manners and was in many ways the nicest friend we knew.

Further gardens clothed the slope leading down to the iron Victoria Bridge, arched above the Wye. Rustic seats were provided. The river proved a major attraction and we spent many happy hours walking along its banks. The Green itself was a popular place for a stroll and the citizens of Hereford took advantage of it most fine days. Among them was an elderly gentleman who took a shine to Nana. Whenever she appeared he would doff his hat and pass the time of day. Such encounters always made Nana blush and 'Nana's gentleman' became a family joke. Far more embarrassing was the ebullient Mr Bustin, the photographer, whose studio stood close to the cathedral west front. He was small and neatly dressed with a white moustache and would always greet Nana effusively. 'How are you, Aunty?' he would cry from afar, as she tried to push past. 'You are looking simply marvellous today!' So Nana in her late fifties had her admirers, though she treated them all with disdain. I used to admire the photographs of prize Hereford bulls whenever we passed Bustin's. In many ways he was Hereford's best known character, that rare kind of cheerful person whom it made you feel better to meet. Everyone knew Bustin and Bustin knew everybody. To look at he resembled 'Mr Pastry', a former popular performer on children's television.

After crossing the Victoria Bridge you could either turn left, following the long since removed white railings, as we called the concrete fence, making for Dinedor, or right across the Bishop's Meadow to the old Wye bridge and the boat club beyond. Nana was very fond of animals, and on one occasion hurried down from the Green to remonstrate with a crowd of urchins chasing sheep.

The dark wooded slopes of Dinedor loomed on the skyline down river from Hereford. One day my parents decided to visit the hill and camp. They took Jack and me with them, though it was a considerable walk. I must have been about three at the time and remember little about it apart from being lifted up by my father into the bole of an old beech. The beech was still there when I returned to Dinedor with my wife more than half a century later. Jack disgraced himself on the return journey by snapping up a baby chicken outside a farm. When my mother reported the incident to the farmer's wife, she was outraged when she charged her seven and six, arguing that the chick would in time become a hen.

A favourite walk was up Aylestone Hill and on to the Tile Works. I don't know whether the latter still exists, but the Hill wasn't the race track it has unfortunately become today. We used to glance enviously at the big houses with their spacious gardens at the top of the Hill and in Hafod Road. But I infinitely preferred walks that led towards the river.

One was to Hampton Bishop. After walking down St Owen Street you came to the railway bridge. There I recall discussing with Nana a recent train accident and opining that it was certainly the signaller's fault. When or where the disaster occurred I do not remember, though it might have been during the war. More memorable was the occasion when my attention was arrested by the sight of a man in uniform holding up a salmon, which he had caught under the bridge.

'I expect he's going to throw it back,' Nana prognosticated. I was somewhat taken aback by the finality of this announcement, being unaware that salmon were the quarry of the privileged and that if an unauthorised person caught a salmon he was required to return it to the river or run the risk of being 'summonsed', which in Nana's view represented the utmost rigour of the law.

Once we walked almost to Mordiford and watched a band of willow strippers at work, presumably gathered the withies for basketwork, but I don't remember witnessing this activity again.

But all our excursions were not so happy. Nana had taken us out for a walk along the road to Hampton Bishop, past the bridge where the soldier caught the salmon. It was a hot summer day so she had packed up a picnic in a basket,

Aylestone Hill.

which she carried with my two baby sisters in the pram. Her original intention
was for us to eat our lunch by the roadside, but chancing to see an open gate
leading into a field she pushed the pram inside and began to unwrap the meal.
At the time I had very little experience of fields, apart from the turf of the
Castle Green and was dismayed to find it filled with tough weeds and thistles
which sorely pricked bare legs. Undeterred, Nana made a place for her charges
by the hedge and spread out a mack to sit on. As usual she had packed all the
things we liked, cold milk and jam sandwiches as well as a few cakes. We were
all beginning to enjoy the excursion when suddenly a trap drew up. It was the
type of high two wheeled vehicle favoured by farmers and the driver was a
typical example of his kind. He was wearing tweeds and a trilby hat cocked to
one side.

'Out o' there', he blazed. 'Or I'll put this whip about you!' My brother and I
were horrified, while my sisters began to cry. Nana stood her ground, pale and
contemptuous, her eyes blazing with rage.

'Upon my word', she answered. 'We're doing no harm.' But the farmer
interrupted her. 'Off my land this minute or I'll . . .' Once again he waved his
whip. Realising that there was nothing to be gained by further argument Nana
repacked the basket, replaced my sisters in the pram and set off for the gate. On
regaining the road she turned round briefly and faced the man in the trap.

'You rude man!' she thundered. 'Frightening the children too!' But her righteous indignation was wasted on the mottle-faced rustic and we duly returned to the road. I had never met an angry farmer before, and was thoroughly unnerved by the experience. There is something about the possession of land which brings out the worst in men. Since then I have avoided trespass and, whenever possible, stick to the right of way.

On another occasion I was taken to a farm outside the city where a group of women was working. Who took me, and why, I do not recall, nor what the women were up to. At some point I was led off by a youth to visit an adjacent orchard. Putting a finger to his lips, as if to warn me that he was about to do something improper, he suddenly grasped a bough heavily laden with apples and shook the fruit to the ground. He generously handed me one to take back, but it wasn't until we rejoined the women that I realised I'd been guilty of theft.

'Where did you get them apples from, John?' a thin beldam with a crafty face simpered. 'They'll be sending a policeman after you.'

Her words made me feel uncomfortable. It was the first time, apart from the farmer, that I had come into contact with country folk and I found them rather frightening. I little realised that we were soon destined to move to the country and to have first hand experience of country ways.

We didn't confine our walks to the Castle Green or Hampton Bishop. White Cross Road was also a favourite where I liked to run up and down the stone steps surrounding the monument. More interesting was walking through Broad Street, over the river and up Ross Road. The attraction for me was the railway bridge, under which, if you were fortunate, trains thundered. I had been a train and locomotive addict ever since I first visited Hereford station, but the Ross Road bridge was more exciting than the station because the engines, trucks and rolling stock were in motion. The fascination of trains and engines for boys and men is curious. A steam engine is admittedly impressive, a fiery creature belching smoke, which it is hard to believe is not alive. So strong in fact is the attraction of steam engines that lines have been revived by enthusiasts for them to run on. And if that weren't sufficient, engines and coaches have been repainted in the old company colours. Britishers and in particular the English are romantics at heart and prepared to pay for a ride in a train drawn by a pre-war engine, on a journey which often leads nowhere. The enthusiasm for opening up former lines is growing and is beginning to spread all over the world.

I must be one of the few people old enough to have travelled on the railways before they were grouped in 1923. Indeed I could probably claim a record in that I made use of no less than four. I have already described how I went first by the Great Western and later by the London and North Western to Abergavenny. But I travelled on the Midland too and the London and South

Western. The Midland Railway ran a line from Hereford to Brecon. It was an attractive route, used by farmers and people from the remoter western regions. One summer day my father decided to go on a family outing to Ladylift, a hilltop overlooking Moorhampton station. Who told him about Ladylift I cannot imagine, but the suggestion was prophetic since we were shortly to live on the far side of that hill. I was fascinated by the red tank engine and carriages, contrasting with the familiar green and brown of the Great Western.

There was only one stop before Moorhampton and that was at Credenhill. When we arrived at Moorhampton Ladylift loomed half a mile distant, the end of a scarp covered with trees, not unlike Dinedor. After crossing a field we climbed up the track, which was masked with bracken, and finally gained the summit. When the picnic was produced the flies descended and swiftly rendered life intolerable. Jack the terrier suffered worst and bit till he was tired at the black plague settling on his muzzle. After vain attempts to ward the flies off with fronds of bracken we gave them best and returned to Moorhampton to await the next train.

I travelled on the London and South Western railway when, during the summer of 1919, we went to stay in Devon. My family were Devonians on my father's side and my aunt and uncle ran the Sidmouth steam laundry. I don't recall much of the visit except playing with the steering wheels of the laundry vans and being frightened by a group of youths celebrating with torches and fire-crackers. What were they celebrating? I have often wondered.

My uncle Harry was a tall, good-looking merry soul, the opposite of my father. Whereas my father was nervy, serious-minded and religious Harry was as bubbling over with fun as a kettle constantly on the boil. Both were tall, though Harry was the taller, and both wore small moustaches. But there the resemblance ended. Their father had been the proprietor of the still well-known White Hart hotel at Moretonhampstead at a time when it offered shooting 'over many thousand acres', and both had briefly attended boarding school. When their father died after neglecting his business his sons were obliged to strike out on their own. Yet their grandfather had served and been close to Lord Devon, who had rewarded him with the Sands Hotel at Slapton (destroyed when troops manoeuvred there during World War II) and subsequently the White Hart. His son married a daughter of the proprietor of the Oxenham Arms at South Zeal, so the family was well represented in the trade.

My favourite walk of all was along Belmont Road, which might seem surprising. There was certainly little to interest a small boy as he tramped along the high pavement. The point was that I had been told that the road led to Abergavenny, where I spent so many holidays with my cousins and enjoyed climbing the local hills. Abergavenny, to my childish mind, represented the very Mecca of adventure and I was always excited by the prospect of going there. Besides, my relations lived in attractive country houses with pleasant gardens and fabulous views. My aunt Ada, my mother's eldest sister, was always game for anything in the nature of a mountain ramble. When tackling the big Skirrid, we trained to the Junction, but the Sugar Loaf and Blorenge were always approached on foot.

One day in spring Edith's successor, a gaunt girl named Ivy, took my brother and me to Dinmore Woods. The purpose of the exercise was to view the daffodils, which were reputed to grow there. The genuine wild daffodil *Narcissus pseudonarcissus* is confined, except where it has been introduced, to very few counties, one of which is Herefordshire. It is shorter than its domestic cousins, but simpler and more lovely. But the woods were bare when the bus dropped us, with never a daffodil in sight. Do wild daffodils still grace Dinmore Woods, I wonder? Daffodils or not, Herefordshire is a delightful county. During the twenties it remained virtually unspoiled. I was exceedingly lucky to be brought up from an early age in such a favoured region, including the city itself with the Castle Green and its other unrivalled amenities. At a time when walking was the normal means of progress Hereford was an excellent centre for excursions. Of course life was different then, when there was little traffic and crime on the modern scale was virtually unknown. It was a time, long past, when the old and the very young could range abroad without fear. There were plenty of police about on the beat by night and day, so everyone felt safe and mothers didn't worry if their children were late.

In a city like Hereford, then unaffected by industry, the bigger social problems didn't arise. The worst that could happen was a man getting drunk or a minor disturbance, perhaps, at the fair. Killings of the kind so common today, like stabbings and shootings were unknown. I vaguely recall the Armstrong murder, when an ex-officer poisoned his wife, but such events excited enormous publicity and were fortunately rare. It is easy to survey the past through rosy spectacles, but the fact remains that life was safer. Had it not been so I probably wouldn't have lived to be writing now, since as a child I was given a loose rein.

Policemen in the twenties were respected and even feared, to the point when they were used as bogy-men to frighten errant children. Though the practice was reprehensible it was a salutary method of instilling respect for law and order among the young. Drug-taking and similar social evils were something you read about in books. Many people were poor, but not so poor that they were obliged to break the law to survive.

Another stabilising factor was religion. Everyone was taught and in general believed that if you were wicked you would go to hell, a salutary deterrent which is now sadly missing.

5 Pennies for Buns and Pantomime

I started school in 1920, when I was nearer six than five. My mother had taught me how to make pot hooks and to copy the letters in the alphabet, but I still couldn't spell or write. I was keen to learn and could probably, with instruction, have actually begun reading, but nobody found time. Anyhow, what were schools for?

The only question to be settled was where I was to go. Since neither my father or mother had ever been to one, public primary schools were never considered. My father had been sent away at a very young age to a boarding school at Chepstow and completed his education at Bovey Tracy Grammar school in south Devon. My mother had attended, I think, the Convent at Abergavenny before proceeding to the newly established girls' intermediate school. Then someone suggested Miss Kear's.

Apart from any other consideration Miss Kear's school was eminently accessible. It was in fact in a house in Church Street directly across the way. The fees were modest, in deference to the clientèle, for the school catered largely for tradesmen's children and not for the professional classes. Some of the children I already knew, like Roy and Keith whom we'd met in the Castle Green. Miss Kear was youngish and always wore fashionable clothes. She never seemed to do much teaching herself but relied largely on her assistant, a rather nice looking woman, who was also a war widow. In the light of the latter misfortune it was hard to believe that her name was Mrs Lucky. Starting school is for most children a traumatic event and for me it was especially so. I had led a sheltered existence and hardly come in contact with the seamier side of life. So when a little girl stole my pencil I was nonplussed and upset. Probably she had confused it with her own, but its loss quite ruined my first day.

The schoolroom was dark, with a single window looking out on to a back-yard. It was also airless. From time to time a man in shirt sleeves looked in, whom we were told was the caretaker. Every morning at a quarter to eleven Mrs Lucky would put on her hat and coat and call out 'Pennies for buns!' The buns she bought at Miss Matthews's and distributed them on her return. That was, of course, if you'd remembered your penny. If not, you watched the others eating, making do with a cup of milk. One morning there was a crash like a wall collapsing as the caretaker's infant shattered the cups when he tripped on the tray. 'It hurt!' he lamented, as Mrs Lucky picked him up, while all eyes were directed at the havoc on the floor.

Break over, it was usually spelling again. Spelling was learned from little limp books with a blue cover, which I hated more and more. There were also sums, which I could rarely do, and switching about with a pointer on the blackboard to make sure we knew our letters. In the end we began to read, though my progress was funereal. We sat on chairs at tables: I still remember the names of my fellow pupils. To begin with I was put to sit alongside a boy with the unforgettable name of Jimmy Dufty. Then there was John Rogers, a good looking dark boy, plump and jolly Rene Smith, the chemist's daughter, the inseparable friends Dorothy Burghall and Mary Kilgour, Roy Willetts and Keith Sinclair whom I've already mentioned, Dennis Brewer, the possessor of impeccable manners who, on one happy occasion, shared a dragon ride with us at the May Fair, Muriel who giggled at everything I said, and silent but beautiful Eileen Corner. Most children were aged between five and eight, with the exception of Mary Edwards and Sally Wood. Mary was the daughter of our neighbours the ironmongers and appeared to the rest of us virtually grown up. So was Sally, who at the mature age of twelve took us for sums. I suppose she was a pupil teacher, for whom both then and later I had the highest regard. Like other apprentices they learned their trade from actual experience and not from lectures delivered at second hand in a college hall. Was she too young to teach at twelve? We certainly didn't think so. After all Cardinal Wolsey is reputed to have graduated MA at Oxford when he was eleven, while recently we have had the example of the remarkable Ruth Lawrence and the Chinese boy of seven. Do we leave everything till we are too old? Such instances suggest it.

Once a week an elderly woman came to teach us French. She was French herself and always wore a heavy costume above several tiers of skirts. All I recall learning were the numbers from one to ten, which I suppose was a start, if not particularly enterprising. What an elderly French woman was doing in Hereford I have often wondered. Probably she was a retired teacher from some girls' school.

Some would argue that private schools are socially divisive. So they may be, but so is society itself. It is also true that some of the teachers they employ are unqualified, but I still put my money on Sally Wood. Private schools have one advantage over state schools in that their classes are usually smaller. Few would have maintained that Miss Kear's was a good school, but you did at least know everyone in it and, what was even more to the point, I was happy there.

One day Miss Kear decided that we should all learn to swim. The place selected for our initiation was the city swimming bath. The existence of the bath was news to me since I had never heard it previously mentioned. Neither of my parents were swimmers, but few were in those days. The swimming bath unfortunately possessed one serious defect. It had been designed for adults and even the shallow end was too deep for children of our age to touch the bottom.

Mrs Lucky, who had been put in charge of swimming, disengaged each terrified child in turn as it clung to the rail and did her best to persuade it to go through the motions of the breast stroke while she clung on to its legs. After a session of spluttering and shrieking the protesting child was restored to the safety of the rail. Discipline at school was good and few pupils caused trouble. A notable exception was when a boy sportively threw another boy's cap up on a roof where he couldn't reach it. When she heard about it Miss Kear immediately instructed Mrs Lucky to call at the police station after she'd finished buying buns. Of course Mrs Lucky did nothing of the kind, but kept up the pretence by announcing on her return that they would be sending a constable round 'in half an hour'. The effect on the pupils was devastating. Nothing could be worse than the arrival of a policeman, which might even end in being 'summonsed'. When no policeman arrived the class relaxed, but the cap thrower had received a salutary warning. The mere threat of the arrival of a policeman was enough to bring shivers.

The most notable event during my time at the school was the production of a pantomime, *Cinderella*. For weeks, we practised singing 'Coal Black Mammy', one of the latest pop songs, accompanied by someone on the piano. Since the rehearsals took place in Miss Kear's flat, perhaps she was the accompanist too. The performance was billed as taking place at the Kemble in Broad Street, Hereford's most prestigious theatre. Keith Sinclair and I were members of the chorus and our respective mothers were kept busy providing suitable clothes. As the period chosen was the eighteenth century the principals paraded in powdered wigs, while Keith and I wore white breeches and black three-cornered hats. Apart from singing in the background we were required to line up on either side of the principals in the finale and were coached in the show room at the Bon Marché on how to divide off. In the end both Keith's and my mother were satisfied that we had mastered what for small boys was a difficult manoeuvre and we looked forward to the day when we should appear on the stage.

Miss Kear was Cinderella and Mrs. Lucky the principal boy. As a consequence the performance attracted a considerable audience with my mother, Emmie and Nana occupying front seats. In addition to the main play, when Mrs Lucky gazed into Miss Kear's eyes and warbled soulfully 'If you were the only girl in the world', a boy and a girl danced a gavotte. The girl was Rene's sister and I immediately fell in love with her, and the boy was Roy Slatter.

Keith and I succeeded in dividing off correctly during the finale and ended

31

up in a line facing the audience. When bouquets were handed up from the orchestra pit to the leading performers Emmie didn't forget me. I received what was then known as a 'dorothy bag' of chocolates, a neat paper carton tied up with ribbon. It would be nice to say that I became a famous actor, whereas my histrionic abilities never extended beyond the school play.

One of the most familiar ways of distinguishing or advertising a school is for the pupils to wear caps and blazers. During the twenties boys at the Hereford Cathedral School wore caps with alternate gold and blue rings. The High School boys wore caps with rings of red and blue though after World War II the wearing of headgear of any description declined. Even Eton abandoned the custom of wearing top hats, though they still retain morning suits as a mark of distinction. Preparatory School boys wore grey felt hats with a coloured band tied round them. Girls' hats varied. The girls at the High School wore close-fitting Tudor style bonnets in winter and broad-brimmed straw hats in summer. All boaters and straw hats were emblazoned with ribbons printed in the appropriate school colours, while caps had cloth squares sewn above the peak decorated with the school arms.

To be in the fashion Miss Kear declared that boys at the school should wear floppy felt hats. Furthermore the hats were to be banded with a length of ribbon coloured red and black. The cost of the ribbon was two and tenpence halfpenny, considered extortionate by some. What girls had to wear I cannot remember, but the pupils attending Miss Kear's academy were now distinguishable in town.

One afternoon I walked up White Cross Road to meet a friend for tea. We recognised one another afar off, since we were both wearing the new school hats. So hats had their advantage, if only for the purpose of recognising a friend. Nowadays few schoolchildren are required to wear headgear of any description, and even uniform is disappearing.

When my sisters were born my mother engaged Alice. Alice was a young woman of I suppose five and twenty with a wall eye. Her parents were poor and lived in Maylord Street behind the Bon Marché. Alice possessed patience and a way with children. She had once gone on an excursion to London Zoo and I used to question her closely about the animals she'd seen. She did her best to pretend she'd seen the most outlandish beasts, which I found in a book called *Noah's Ark*. Neither she nor I knew that the animals in question weren't in the zoo, while one, the quagga, was actually extinct.

We all loved Alice who in addition to helping with the household chores frequently took us for walks. Like Christopher Robin's Alice she too had a suitor, though a workman called Jim, not a soldier. Returning one evening from an outing with Alice a disturbance in Eign Street attracted my attention. Two policemen were struggling with a man lying in the road and even as I watched one lost his helmet. It rolled into the gutter among the crowd which had gathered to watch the fun. But it wasn't fun at all, it was a young man suffering an epileptic fit and suddenly Alice shouted 'It's my brother!'

I have never forgotten seeing him writhing there, with a trickle of saliva foaming on his lips. Hitherto I had had no contact with serious illness, but worse was to follow when I took a stroll with my mother in the Castle Green. A rowing boat was moving slowly up and down the Bishop's Pool, with a man leaning out with a what looked like a pole, till I observed the hook at the end and assumed it was a gaff.

'Look! someone's caught a salmon!' I observed to my mother who turned round to watch. In fact several people were watching and I heard one of them say 'They're dragging the river.' The meaning of the phrase was lost on me, but when my mother said 'I shall be sick if they bring up the body,' I realised it was something awful. Fortunately we didn't stay to test my mother's words, but it was certainly my first acquaintance with death.

Less harrowing was an extraordinary scene of which Roy Willetts and I were the sole witnesses, once again in the Castle Green. A party of young people suddenly appeared fighting around a pram. In the pram was a baby and as we watched the mother who was pushing it broke into a run. The others followed, shouting and struggling until they were lost to view. When I got home I reported the occurrence to my parents who were, at first, as baffled as Roy and I. Later my father found an account of the incident in the Hereford Times, from which it appeared that it had all been a domestic dispute.

6 Exclusive of Salmon

I was five when I took up fishing. I know, because my father informed an acquaintance as we were walking through the Cathedral Close that I was six. But I wasn't. My birthday fell in April and it was still only March. Someone had told my father that fishing was good for the nerves. If you wanted to take up fishing then you could hardly have lived in a more convenient place. The Wye was only a short walk away, across the Castle Green. The Wye, from a fishing point of view, was no ordinary river. The salmon were renowned throughout the land, and though salmon were not our quarry there were plenty of roach, dace and trout. When I grew up salmon became my quarry, but in Wales, never on the Herefordshire Wye.

My father started fishing with a roach pole and confined his activities to coarse fishing. During this phase he invited old Mills to join him and I well recall drawing their attention to a chub lying in a pool below the reach normally reserved for swimming. They failed to catch it, or indeed anything else, but my father wasn't always so unsuccessful and often caught roach. He once got into a fish which ran off down river taking all his line. In the end it got off and I have always suspected that it was not a salmon, but a pike.

I wanted a rod too and dabbled about in the shallows with a worm fishing for minnows. I didn't bother with hooks, but when a fish took the bait I flung it over my head. Who, I wonder, bothers to eat minnows to-day? Nana fried them and they tasted like sardines. When my father graduated from coarse, that is using float and bait, to fly fishing he gave me the roach rod. This as things turned out was a bad mistake. One morning, accompanied by my three year old brother, I put the rod down on the bank while I went to examine the state of the water. When I returned the rod had gone. 'A boy took it', my brother explained. When my father found out he was naturally annoyed and told me 'You'd better go and look for it!' The futility of this advice struck me even then, though I made a pretence of obeying it.

Fishing at Hereford was not free. Membership of the local angling association cost ten shillings and six pence a season, though I was exempted as a boy. But that wasn't all. You had to purchase a licence issued by the Board of Conservators, though I have often wondered what they did with the money. A salmon licence cost three pounds, which put it out of reach of all but the well to do. My father bought a trout licence which cost half a crown, bearing the warning EXCLUSIVE OF SALMON. I was immensely proud of my shilling green coarse fishing permit, inscribed with my name and address, and eager to produce it on demand. But, to my disappointment, nobody ever asked to see

34

it, or even my father's buff coloured trout licence. He might have found himself in trouble when he filled his bag, in all innocence, with salmon smolts, known locally as 'pink'.

In comparison with the cost of fishing today such fees must appear derisory. But then wages and incomes were only a fraction of what they are now and the fees reflected it. Even so they were far from being regarded as negligible by those required to pay them and I am reminded how when, a year or two later, I inquired of a man at Glasbury whether the fishing was free he regarded me for a moment with a look of pitying contempt before growling, 'No fishing's free 'ere. I pays 'alf a dollar'.

The chief tackle shop in Hereford was kept by the Hatton brothers. They didn't confine their business to fishing, but were also a games and athletic store as well as boot and shoe makers. To begin with, Hattons' was far too grand for me and I preferred to patronise old Williams who managed Philip Morris's, the ironmonger and gunsmith. Morris's shop was in Widemarsh Street. Old Williams was a delightful person endowed with infinite patience, especially when dealing with small boys. Not even the paltry order for a penny worth of fly-gut or a threepenny golden spinner was beneath his attention, though he would sometimes grin wryly and sigh. He was a big man with a small fair moustache and a kindly Welsh accent. I did business with old Williams for many years and have never forgotten him. I also did business with Hattons', but that was later.

My father's favourite stretch on the Wye was the pebble beach below the Victoria Bridge. It was a good place for casting and for catching smolts. Smolts, young salmon feeding in the river prior to quitting it for the sea, will snatch at anything as my father soon discovered. Trout are far more wily. If you catch a smolt you are bound to return it, but this is easier said than done. It is often difficult to remove the fly, when the hook is deeply embedded. Still catching 'pink' made my father's day, until he learned better.

The prolonged drought of 1921, which turned the grass on the Green brown, also had its effect on the Wye, several of whose stretches were reduced to a trickle. The pebble beach grew wider and wider and one day my father hooked a chub. It came bouncing across the stony strand like a small salmon. A chub is not much of a catch and is normally disdained by experienced anglers, but my father had never hooked one before or indeed any fish approaching it in size.

Nobody seemed to worry when my brother and I set out on our own for the river. It was true that by then we had become familiar with its surroundings, but either my parents were too busy to worry or they simply didn't appreciate the possible dangers we faced. These didn't include (in those days) kidnap, killing or rape, though on one occasion I was persuaded by a trampish

The river Wye and the Victoria Bridge from Castle Green.

individual to sit on his lap. However, I managed to escape, but never told my parents what had happened. During a time of full employment few anglers appeared on the river until the evening, so that there was nobody to notice or interfere with the actions of such as my assailant.

The river dropped so low that it was reduced to a series of pools linked by swift streams. At one point above the bathing stretch it appeared actually fordable. Holding my brother's hand I waded through the shallows until I reached the torrent. It dragged at our legs, but we weren't deterred and arrived safe on the opposite bank. Our crossing was witnessed by an acquaintance who told my father that he had feared to shout a warning in case it distracted us. I don't know whether anyone else waded the Wye that season, but there is no doubt that it was a hazardous thing to do. During the evenings fishermen would stand on the Victoria Bridge and fish for gudgeon. Gudgeon are small fish of the carp family with filaments hanging from the mouth. They are said to be good eating, though I never caught any. I used to amuse the men when I wished them 'Good luck!' in passing. The only regular angler I recall was named Walter. He wore a straw boater festooned with artificial flies, and after selecting one he would fairly lash the water. His expertise impressed me, as well as the speed with which he hooked trout. His normal beat was above the bridge and he almost always waded. As for salmon I don't remember ever seeing anyone fishing for them, but that was probably because we fished mostly in summer. The salmon anglers would have been out in early spring or autumn, but it seems strange that I never saw them even then. Perhaps they ignored the Association water and confined their activities to the higher stretches of the river.

Now that I had become an accredited angler Emmie made me a fishing bag. It included a proper division for the fish and I was so proud of it that I wore it on every possible occasion. We didn't always fish the Wye. One day my father decided to take the train to Moreton and try his luck on the Lugg. The Lugg joins the Wye near Mordiford, but is in every respect an inferior river. To begin with it holds few trout, except in the higher reaches, and is innocent of salmon. On the other hand it held plenty of dace and, what appealed to my youthful imagination, a great store of pike, the so-called 'sharks of the river', known colloquially as 'jack'. I was most insistent that my father should catch a pike, but being inexpert in that branch of fishing his efforts remained un-rewarded. Not so the father of one of our shopgirls named Daniels. He was short and fresh-faced with a drooping moustache. He wore blue overalls and a broad peaked cloth cap. He had already landed several jack by the time we arrived, which lay snapping and gasping on the bank. Every so often he would give them a kick to see whether they were still alive. I have seen salmon fishers treat their catches in this reprehensible fashion, but even as a boy I strongly disapproved. Nevertheless my father bought a pike which I carried home in triumph. I believe some consider pike a delicacy, despite their feeding habits. Nana had never baked a pike before and spent some time studying Cassell's *Dictionary of Cookery*. I looked forward to the meal with growing impatience, but one mouthful was enough and I was promptly sick.

Suddenly there came the news that old Mills had resolved to sell the shop. It appeared that he had received an offer from his old firm Lloyds Bank and as a former servant he thought he ought to accept it. My father considered that it would be far more profitable to put such a desirable premises up for auction, with wealthy firms like Woolworth's and Marks & Spencers in view. But the old man remained adamant and in due course the shop was sold.

So my father decided to look out for another business, preferably in the country. Unfortunately, impetuosity was his second name and he closed with an offer in an out of the way village where the commercial possibilities were bound to be limited. Ironically, Lloyds Bank delayed their occupation of the Hereford premises for several years so we could have stayed where we were and avoided any hasty decision. The effect of this was particularly evident later when I had to travel daily by train to Hereford to school.

The author kitted out with fishing bag accompanied by his younger brother.

7 Weobley Docks

None of us had ever heard of Weobley till my father decided to move there. It lay in a remote rural backwater, twelve miles north-west of Hereford. Approached by a minor road, the nearest railway station was three and a half miles away, while the sole means of transport was by horse brake. It was literally cut off by snow in winter, while it roasted in the summer heat. It had once been a famous town, which sent two members to parliament, but the Reform Act had put an end to its consequence and the fine mansions which had housed the aristocratic voters had long since been pulled down. We knew nothing of this and drove off in a taxi, followed by a furniture van, to the exciting prospect of living in the country.

There is no denying that Weobley, with its wealth of black and white houses, was, and still is, one of the most picturesque villages in Britain. The arrival of newcomers didn't go unremarked and the empty street soon filled with children. I remember a little girl standing in the road wearing a white pinafore and looking like a doll. Parents, meantime, watched from behind window curtains, wondering who we were. When I say we, I include Nana and Emmie, as well as the terrier Jack. Dear old Jack! He was destined to remain our close companion for upwards of fourteen years, and this despite overfeeding by Nana until he could scarcely waddle, and people poked fun at him whenever he appeared. I would expect to receive a warm welcome from Jack in the next world, if there is a next world, and if dogs inhabit it.

My brother Tom and I were enormously impressed by the garden, which was long and narrow and included a big shed. The shed was an ancient building which, as some of the older residents remembered, had once housed itinerant tailors. It boasted a long since glassless window and was built on two storeys with a stone stair leading up to the top. The bottom was used for storing fuel and also for housing fowls. Keeping fowls was an exciting new hobby. The top storey contained a bench and wooden vice where I passed happy hours making boats.

The garden couldn't hold a candle to the Castle Green, but Fred Hope's meadow beyond the top wall could. It wasn't very big as meadows go, but still large enough to accommodate a football pitch while beyond, over a stile, was a pond. The pond, for some enigmatic reason, was known as the Bear Croft while the Hopes' house in the village was called the Bear. Had it once been connected with bear bating? More probably the Bear was originally an inn. You approached the meadow through a wooden door which we were strictly charged to keep locked to prevent an invasion of sheep or cattle, which

39

T.C. Pollard's shop and Manley's grocery opposite the Red Lion Inn, Weobley.

happened on at least one occasion. A ram lamb was kept as a pet by Fred's daughter Mabel and was great fun before he grew up. He then became a serious menace, challenging all and sundry who dared to cross his path. But all this was to come.

We were fortunate in our neighbours the Manleys who kept the adjacent grocer's shop. They were Quakers and cultured people with a daughter away at school. Behind the grocer's shop was a series of outbuildings as well as an orchard. Later, when the game became popular, the Manleys followed the example of the Red Lion Hotel opposite and laid out a tennis lawn. My father and mother were keen players and we soon became adept ourselves. The lawn and orchard were used for garden fêtes and parties. As for the shop, it was small in comparison with the Bon Marché, but included an annexe, known as the Boot Room. The house, on the other hand, was distinctly roomy, with five bedrooms, lounge, dining room and kitchen, but no bathroom since there was no running water in the village. We were obliged to use a pump. The house wasn't black and white like the others, having suffered conversion at a later date.

We arrived on a bright February day in 1922, the year when the parliamentary back-bench committee was founded. I was still only seven, rising eight, while my brother was five and my sisters still infants. It was time for elevenses and Emmie took us up to Tait's, the combined grocer's and baker's at the top of the street, to inquire whether they sold buns. They had run out as it happened, but the tall handsome man in charge offered us oranges. Later we learned that he was one of three bachelor brothers and a musical genius. Next we called at a cottage in search of milk. It was a novel experience to go out and buy milk instead of having it delivered at the door. During our peregrinations I was struck by the strange silence, caused by the virtual absence of traffic. The shop stood in Broad Street, the main thoroughfare, and was styled somewhat grandly 'Manchester House'.

The village itself was built on a slope leading down from the grassy humps of a medieval border castle. It had been active during the internecine struggles between Queen Maud and Stephen, but was already in ruins by the time of Elizabeth. The church at the bottom was a splendid edifice, with a tall, narrow steeple.

A mile or so beyond the castle ruins was a modern castle, called Garnstone, at the foot of an escarpment, known as the 'ill. Dropping aspirates was a common feature of rustic speech in Herefordshire and in particular in the western parts of the county. Aspirates, on the other hand, were often supplied irrationally to words like owl and edge, which were pronounced howl and hedge. The hill was long and heavily wooded, ending in Ladylift, the scene of our earlier visit. Above the castle stretched the park, which supported a herd of deer. The owner of the castle was William Verdin, known as Al' Billy.

Manchester House was lighted by gas. The gas was supplied by carbide delivered in large drums. The gasworks itself was in a shed alongside the kitchen. The first night of our arrival my father went in to examine it, only to emerge with a sea-green face and on the point of collapse. In the end he got the hang of it, but soon took steps to switch to electricity.

At the bottom of the hill below the shop was a circular concrete horse trough, known as the tank. It was associated with a curious piece of folklore, as I learned when I went back to Hereford to school. To my surprise I was constantly referred to as the one who swept the tide out at Weobley Docks. Nobody in the village ever used the phrase, which must have gone out of usage when the stream was piped beneath the tank and no longer had to be forded. Possibly in times of heavy rain it presented a minor hazard for coaches and other horse-drawn vehicles, though the source of the joke appears to have been forgotten.

Having arrived in the country we lost no time in acquiring pets, a pleasure which had been denied us in town. Hearing of a Belgian hare down Kington Road which required a good home I went down and bought it. It was owned by the Davies family, with whose sons, Curly and Johnny, I was soon to

Weobley Docks.

become acquainted. After receiving instructions on how to clean out a hutch, I returned with the rabbit in a basket. The trouble was fodder, so when the spring came I was sent out to gather herbs and wild parsley.

There is no spring like a first spring and I was soon revelling in the flowers and birds. Primroses and violets seemed to grow everywhere, while bird song was all about. I soon took an interest in birds and learned to distinguish them using *Birds shown to the Children*, which someone had given me as a present. I'd never seen a chaffinch till I came to Weobley and there they were pecking about the road. Then there were rooks in a spinney not far from the old castle as well as jackdaws nesting in the church tower. They were soon joined by swifts, while swallows hawked round the ponds and martins built their mud homes under the eaves.

All this was exciting and made up for the fishing I had enjoyed on the Wye. True, a brook ran close by the village, but effluent from the workhouse which stood on its bank had proved a deterrent to trout. They still survived in the lower reaches, some miles further down. So fishing was out, at least for the time being, and birding was in.

It didn't take me long to realise that the people of Weobley differed markedly from our friends in the town. The latter, by comparison, were sophisticated and articulate, unlike the villagers who were rough mannered and inclined to be hostile to strangers in their midst. Our veneer of respectability constituted a handicap when we tried to make friends. Farmers were a race apart and took a deal of knowing. Another distinct handicap was the possession of books. Only the vicar and the Methodist minister owned books, and the wider knowledge which they brought me merely roused the jealousy of my companions. This was particularly obvious when I aired my knowledge of birds in the presence of gamekeepers' sons.

Countrymen aren't scientists, concerned with the accuracy of identification, but this was a lesson I was long in learning. One of the most interesting features of the Weobley populace was that the majority had Welsh names. Davies, Morgan, Matthews, Lewis, Griffith and Jones were two a penny and not seldom related. This did not prevent them from quarrelling, but they'd always band together against a stranger. The latter was not infrequently me and I duly paid the penalty. Weobley's had been a border castle built to repel Welsh invaders. Were the villagers the descendants of the survivors of a successful raid or of prisoners taken in the fighting? Whatever the truth of the matter the inhabitants of Weobley regarded themselves as English, and anyone with a Welsh accent became a figure of fun.

All names weren't Welsh. A good Herefordshire name was Hope, which is a place name and borne by two farmers. A local squire was Dent, and there were Pudges, Nashes and Berrys as well. But nobody in the village troubled about names. To begin with everyone knew everybody and always knew everything that went on. And when I say knew everyone I mean just that. They were not mere acquaintances who passed the time of day, but people who shared problems and were usually prepared to lend a helping hand. This was especially true in an agricultural community when everyone turned to help with the harvest. Poverty is a great leveller and most people were poor, so they always had that in common. But poverty in the country is not the same as poverty in town. In the country nobody starved and nobody took much interest in politics. An exception was when Ben Tillett, the old Labour campaigner, arrived unexpectedly. He sat silent propped up in the seat of a car, looking rather like Gladstone. He was introduced to the crowd by a man named Box who fairly ranted away. Until then I had remained ignorant of politics and parties and was surprised when the fathers of the boys I knew interjected 'Yur, yur!' But Tillett's visit was a one off and I heard no more of politics till the general election.

It is difficult to realise in an era when needy people qualify for some form of national assistance that there was no help forthcoming in the early nineteen twenties. There was only the old age pension of ten shillings a week, for which men qualified when they reached the age of seventy. In general the state didn't help and if you were poor you just went under, which meant going to the workhouse, where you could be clothed and fed. Many children I knew were so poor that their clothes were in tatters and they walked several miles to school. Obliged to dwell in tied cottages with leaky roofs and primitive amenities most labourers' children rarely washed or bathed. Consequently they stank, though you only noticed when they came inside out of the fresh air. Though all children were required by law to attend school, many had to help their parents, before setting out or after returning home. The work was often heavy and dangerous, a foretaste of what they would have to endure in life. I well remember a neighbour's son saying to me 'You never do no work'. It was perfectly true. I didn't have to work because my father was in a position to engage a boy to carry out the less agreeable chores.

We had two in succession. First Thomas, the sixteen year old son of a gamekeeper, followed by Jim. Their main job, before we changed to electricity, was to wheel away the carbide drums, and they also brought in coal, which my father ordered from the station a truck at a time. Thomas disliked being ordered about by Nana, especially when she landed him with menial chores like cleaning out the rabbits, but he loved nothing more that wheeling out my sisters in a pram, when he could gossip with cronies and go where he liked. Jim was very different, being distinctly good looking, with a freckled face and a mop of unruly hair. His father was in charge of the home farm at Garnstone, while his mother was a redhead with a cockney accent who also sang. Jim once escorted Tommy and me back to Ladylift and on our return we had tea with his mother. Jim was only fifteen, but was a gifted pianist and could play from ear any tune you liked, as a result of which he was in constant demand during the visits of a mobile cinema. On this occasion he accompanied his mother as she rendered the popular ditty 'Yes, we have no bananas.' My brother and I were most amused when she pronounced say as sigh and day as die. Nevertheless it was clear that Jim derived his talents from his mother.

Jim possessed not only musical talents, he was also a born electrician and mechanic. In those days everyone lighted their bicycle lamps with carbide at night, but Jim went one better. He tied a small dynamo to his front wheel and so lit his lamp with electricity. My father did well at Weobley to begin with and gave us expensive toys. One was a miniature projector, which Jim was called in to work. He also loved to play with my railway layout, to which he added many inventions of his own. I have often wondered what happened to Jim, a gifted youth with an eye for the girls.

While at Weobley my father took up professional photography and I spent many hours with him in the darkroom fixing plates. He had a large stand camera and was constantly in demand at social functions.

One of the most binding social elements is school, and in particular, as at Weobley, going to the same school. All but a few went to Weobley School except the doctor's children who were sent away. As a result they knew nobody on their return. The few went to Miss Manley's, the local equivalent of Miss Kear's, but the few were very few indeed, including a farmer's and baker's daughter. Miss Manley, unlike Miss Kear, really knew her stuff and I was sent to her to learn French and later for coaching in a number of subjects. In the meantime I went to Weobley School, with little realization of what I was in for. My mother and Nana had protested from the first that I should be sent to Miss Manley's. But my father was adamant and things worked out in a way nobody could have foreseen.

8 The Boss who was God

The village school stood near the end of Broad Street. It was a church foundation, so much time was devoted to hymn singing and prayers. Not so in the girls' half of the playground, where they would form a circle about anyone they chose and sing this ditty. When they reached the line which revealed the boy's name they would shriek it at the top of their voices:

> The wind, the wind, the wind blows high
> The rain comes scattering from the sky.
> He is handsome, she is pretty,
> She's the girl from the golden city.
> Kisses, kisses, one, two, three,
> Pray and tell me who is he –
> Raggy Richards is her lover,
> All the boys are fighting for her.
> Let the boys say what they will,
> Raggy Richards loves her still.

On joining the school I had been put to sit by a pretty little girl in Class III lower, along with the other seven year olds. She was called Edie and had shining brown locks and wide-apart eyes. To my huge embarrassment she told me the first morning that we were engaged. Worse, a few days later I noticed the girls glancing mischievously across the wooden fence, which divided the playgrounds, straight in my direction. In no time at all a ring was formed with Edie in the centre. I pretended not to notice, but when they shrieked my name I hared incontinently for the lavatory. There was no refuge there. A big-un, as the senior boys were known, seized me by the collar shouting 'D'ya know, Pinkie, 'ow us kills ship?' I didn't, but I soon learned. After screwing his finger painfully under my ear for upwards of five minutes he grew tired of the pastime and let me go, but only into the grasp of another big-un who commanded me fiercely to pull a face. He was a rather good-looking youth like the merciless villain in the cowboy film. I did my best to comply, but not to his satisfaction and in the end he too released me.

It soon became evident that I had learned less than nothing at the dame's. I couldn't spell or read, while the simplest sums defeated me. We used slates and if we talked in class we were punished by being kept in and made to write a hundred times 'I must not talk'. The futility of this exercise should have been patent to everyone except the teachers, who merely conformed to the general

Broad Street, Weobley.

practice. We learned to spell by syllables, a method which has no superior. When I moved from Class III into the 'big room', spelling was practised every morning by each pupil standing up and repeating in turn.

'See, oh, en – con,' Margaret, a bright girl would recite. 'Ess, tea, ar, you, see, tea – struct. Tea, eye, oh, en – shun – construction.' Very occasionally a pupil misheard the word he or she was told to spell. 'See, aitch, eye, em – chim,' one boy began hopefully. 'En, eye, en – nin – chimnin.' There is, of course, no such word and the class dissolved in laughter.

The classes at Weobley Parochial School were numbered backwards. Class III was the lowest, apart from the Infants, and Class I, with its appendage for leavers known as top class, the highest. All the classes were subdivided into upper and lower, which were taken by the same teacher. Class III was the charge of the pleasant young Miss Grant, Class II was taught by Miss Lewis, an older and efficient schoolmistress, and the three upper standards by the 'Boss'. I learned most from two patient pupil teachers, little more than girls, both of whom had only recently left the school. Alfred Dean, known universally as the Boss, was a short man with a clipped grey moustache and a highly developed sense of his own importance. 'Some years ago,' he once told us, 'the Kaiser

47

arrived at a school unannounced while driving through Germany. An aide-de-camp hurried in to warn the headmaster that the All Highest had condescended to pay the school a visit. To the aide's amazement the master remained seated in the Kaiser's presence, explaining to his sovereign that it was all important from a disciplinary point of view that his boys shouldn't know that there was anyone greater than he. And the Kaiser had quite agreed with him.' Though the authenticity of the story must remain extremely doubtful it did at least explain Dean's lordly attitude to others. On the credit side Dean was a strict disciplinarian and kept the instrument of punishment, a short thick cane, in the desk in the big room where he sat. Truancy was a heinous crime and when a boy known as Bumper, who lived in a remote cottage in abject poverty, remained at home to help his father when his mother died, Dean marched into Class III when the boy returned and beat him on the hands till he cried. Bumper, who was a tough boy of eight, remained stoical enough after he received the first two cuts, but finally burst into tears with pain when the final strokes landed on his swollen palms. What was worse was the way his little girl classmates winced every time the cane landed. In the end Bumper and his family were consigned to the local workhouse and were for once decently clad.

Dean, of course, had God on his side, and read the lessons each Sunday in church. This was reflected in the excessive attention paid to religion in school, to the point of absurdity. Learning, to his chagrin, on one unforgettable occasion that nobody knew the date or the meaning of our Lord's circumcision, Dean remarked to the senior mistress 'Miss Lewis, remind me. We must have a special lesson on the subject.' What the content of such a lesson could have been in that fig-leaf era baffles the imagination. Happily it never took place.

In addition to hymn singing on arrival in the morning and again before leaving in the afternoon music itself loomed large in the curriculum, but it wasn't music in the ordinary sense. It certainly wasn't the kind you can enjoy, but a kind of music-mathematical exercise with a chart spread over a blackboard, printed with cabbalistic signs. They represented, of course, something called the tonic sol-fa: doh, ray, me, fah, plus all the intervening semi-tones. To me they meant nothing, but kind Miss Grant took pity on my ignorance and would come and stand beside me when the class was being examined by Dean and give me the correct note. In the big room Dean himself would give us the note on the piano when we were required to sing a song, though I never heard him play a complete tune. This made me suspect that he couldn't, unlike my father who could rattle off melodies at will. After giving the note he would raise his cane, conductor fashion, as we attempted to sing some very strange part-time airs.

The chough and crow to roost have gone,
The owwwwwwwwwwwl sits on the tree –

followed by the rousing chorus

Uprouse ye then, my merry, merry men.

There was also a bit about 'The wild fires dance at night!' We never sang an honest chorus like John Peel. Music, like everything else, was subject to discipline.

Exams were termly and did nobody any harm. A curious feature was the marking system. Everything was marked out of three, instead of the more usual ten, so the possible number of marks in an examination comprising seven subjects was twenty-one. The subjects included writing, spelling, composition and arithmetic, as well as history and reading.

Having never heard of bad language in my life I was puzzled by my schoolmates' usage of such phrases as 'needs 'is ass kicked' and, in my innocence, at first imagined that the reference was to some refractory quadruped. Then there were jockeys. 'You gotta 'ave a jockey!' Johnny, a cheery, tiny member of the Davies family, from whom I'd obtained the tame rabbit, informed me one break. I had never heard of jockeys and was unaware that many people spent much of their time studying form and backing horses. One boy, I recall, favoured Smirke, and Johnny the champion Steve Donaghue.

I was equally ignorant of professional football and when my ear screwer bragged about the playground 'Sunderland's got the wind up!' I hadn't the least notion to whom or what he referred. It was I gathered connected with the Cup, of which I knew nothing either.

Popular pastimes among the boys were marbles, downers and tick. The game of marbles, properly played, can be quite complicated. Not so at Weobley school. A pit was scraped in the playground rubble for the reception of marbles flicked from a line. The line, like the pit, was scraped with a boot, with a second line nearer the mark. Since the big-uns were more adept at flicking they soon rooked the smaller boys. It was a primitive pastime which had probably been practised by the villagers for ages. Whether it was unique to Weobley I do not know, but I never came across it again.

Downers was unique to Weobley, at least in the form in which it was played. It was in essence a chase in which all could take part, but in which, owing to the confinement of the area chosen, nobody could be caught. It was played round the block of buildings which stood like an island in the middle of Broad Street, including a baker's which eventually caught fire. The rules were simple. One boy went 'down', normally a big-un, which meant pretending not to look, while the rest ran off and concealed themselves behind the top wall. He then attempted to creep up unseen and grab one of the others, who then took his place. It never worked and the game usually ended with a general stampede back to the start. Tick consisted of sparring with another boy and escaping before he could strike back. Stilts cut from hedges were all the rage at one time, as was playing horses, while everyone collected fag cards, an educative pastime since the subjects ranged from famous portraits to 'Do you know'?

Most exciting of all, not to say frightening, was running round the streets in the dark. A big-un was usually chosen to play fox, while the rest, led by another big-un, went in pursuit. Whenever they drew a blank the latter would cup his hands and bellow ''ollow or the dogs won't follow!' When a reply came from the direction of the churchyard the fox was given best, since everyone believed in ghosts.

'Plenty up our way,' a friend named Eric once informed me. He lived with his grandmother, who did our washing, in a remote spot overlooking the Wye valley called Shoal's Bank. I have often wondered since on what Eric based his evidence.

Almost every boy had a nickname at Weobley school. I was dubbed Polly or Pinkie almost from the day of my arrival, both common sobriquets for Pollard. Baggy was one of the big-uns, but the source of his name is lost. Crower was always whining and getting people into trouble with his formidable and over-protective mother, whereas Bizz, his brother, was a merry soul, good at football and fond of the girls. Punt, pronounced in the northern way, was the postman's son. Punt possessed a ribald wit and was always the lively centre of any knot of youths. There was also Punt, pronounced like the boat, the small quiet son of the driver of a traction engine, who lived on Weobley Marsh.

The Marsh lay a mile from the village. It was a place of smallholders. Why the two Punts were so christened I never discovered, yet the nicknames were curiously appropriate. Curly Davies had a wave in his hair, so the name for once was self explanatory. Why Bumper, the boy who was caned by the Boss, was so called was, like so many others, a mystery. Peck, a serious minded boy, handed out the prayer books at Sunday School, as well as the attendance stamps. Tater was a plump boy and Napus, a Welsh boy. Who first called him Napus I do not know, but somehow the name suited. Goggy was a friendly youth with whom I exchanged birds' eggs, and Bailey, Manley's amiable assistant who worked in the garden next door.

Girls and women were mostly exempt from nicknames apart from Welshy who frightened me out of my life. Welshy was a tomboy who turned cartwheels on her way to school and gave me secret smiles. I was, I suppose, rising nine at the time and still very frightened of girls.

50

In many ways my parents were far more innocent than I was having never been previously exposed to living in the raw. They tended to regard the villagers as middle-class people like themselves and the villagers naturally took advantage of it. I have often wondered how many of the villagers had been married in church or chapel, or whether, as nowadays, they simply lived together. There were certainly very few weddings, though the same couldn't be said of funerals.

When Mrs Dean died the entire school attended the funeral. She was the infants' teacher and her passing was widely mourned. Her death came like a thunderclap because it was so unexpected. Every day children inquired about her health when she was ill and when the news came that she had died everyone was devastated. I had never encountered death before and was deeply affected by the grimness of the whole business. Watching at the graveside while the coffin was lowered and seeing adults weep is not a scene for children.

After his wife's death Dean went away and as a result discipline suffered. In the end the vicar was called in. 'This isn't a bear garden, boys!' he thundered. No-one, of course knew what a bear garden was, but it was a bear garden just the same.

9 Stinging Nettles, Hop-pickers and Fights

One morning in May – it was actually the 29th – I happened to stroll up to the castle ruins before they rang the bell. There were two bells, the first of which acted as a warning and was rung at a quarter to nine, while the second rang at five minutes to the hour when you were expected to check in at school. A posse of big-uns attracted my attention. For some obscure reason they had tied handkerchiefs round their hands and were carrying bunches of greenery. They were also chuckling, and the big-uns rarely laughed unless they were up to some mischief. They were. The bunches of greenery were stinging-nettles and before I could move they had grabbed me. 'Yur's another little-un without an oak-apple!' one of the big-uns chortled. Next moment a bunch of nettles was thrust into my face and I ran off weeping, my face a mass of weals. Just then I heard the second bell so that there was no time to go home and obtain some ointment. Why I had been attacked I did not know, but concluded that the big-uns had invented a new form of bullying.

What I had failed to realise was that May 29 is Oak-apple Day, when the exiled Charles II is supposed to have hidden from his pursuers in an oak in Shropshire. Since then it had become the custom for royalist sympathisers to wear an oak-apple on that day as a badge of loyalty. Neither the youths who had stung me nor I knew this, but the custom must have originated in the distant past. Weobley was royalist during the Civil War and there was a secret hiding place at a local mansion called The Ley for supporters of the Stuarts. I was shown it by Miss Berry, whose uncles farmed the land, since she was friendly with my parents. The Throne Farm, which stood on the corner of the old Hereford road, was said to be where Charles I put up for the night during his wanderings through Wales. The Throne, a long impressive ivy-covered building had been an inn, in fact the original Unicorn Hotel. So the stinging appears to have been founded on tradition. Otherwise it is hard to see how it arose. In future I gathered an oak-apple in time.

Unlike most others Weobley school carried on through the heat of summer, breaking up only on September the first. This was to accommodate the children who went with their parents hop-picking. The nearest hopyards were owned by a bachelor landowner named Dent who lived with his sister at Newton Court, a mile or two from the village. Dent was a typical country gentleman of his time, who was more interested in hunting than farming, so a good deal was grassland, grazed by cattle and a solitary goat. From September on he attended to the hop-pickers, who received payment by tallies which they later exchanged.

Dent's hopyards were extensive, so much so that the village was unable to produce sufficient labour. That was where the Dudleys came in. Dudley is situated in the heart of the Black Country and hop-picking offered a holiday in the country for the workers in the ironworks and their families. As far as I remember the Dudleys camped in the hopyards, which was all very well as long at it was fine. How they got to Weobley I do not know, though I suppose they hired transport.

A further example of my parents' starry eyed innocence was to send me with Bizz's mother to assist with the picking. The knowledge that there were Dudleys there didn't seem to worry them or the certainty that I would be exposed to the language of the gutter.

Hop-picking, I discovered, consisted of gathering the hops, which hung down from the supports, and putting them into a crib. The crib, which was made of sacking, was as big as a large bath. When it was full tellers would come round, measure the crop, put it in bags and hand out the tallies. In the meantime, in order to relieve the tedium the Dudleys sang. And they didn't sing opera. A favourite was

'ere's to the good old beer, mop it down,
'ere's to the good old beer, mop it down.
'ere's to the good old beer, that makes you feel so queer,
'ere's to the good old beer, mop it down.

There were further verses, more vulgar, the significance of which went over my head. The value of such an experience is hard to judge. At least I learned about hop-picking. I was then still only eight.

I learned also about fighting. I hadn't been in the school long when a boy, for no reason, tapped me on the shoulder and told me it was his 'challenge'. What challenge meant I had no idea until someone mentioned fighting. Fighting, I was informed, took place in the street after school. To a sensitive boy this was awful intelligence and when the school ended I declined to leave. Instead I took refuge with the new teacher in Class III (I was then in Class II), a Cornishwoman named Harris, with a strong accent. 'What be the matter with yow?' she demanded, when I pushed nervously through the door. 'They be fighting, Miss,' Crower explained. 'Fighting?' The teacher took time to swallow this bombshell before ordering me to sit down. So the dread day was saved, but only postponed as I was soon to discover.

One evening as I was leaving school I watched a fight between two small boys, which had clearly been provoked by the big-uns. The big-uns rarely

The author with his brother and sisters and assorted pets.

fought one another, preferring the role of promoters. A ring had quickly formed round the two unwilling antagonists to prevent them escaping. They were then launched at one another from behind to the sound of shouts and jeers, much as happened at Eton College in the early years of the last century, only there bets were laid and one boy died. In the end one of the contestants struck the other in the face by accident. The other immediately behaved like a windmill, with his arms flailing the air. Soon they were both at it until one's face crumpled and dissolved into floods of tears. Only then did the ring break up as the big-uns made for home. The defeated warrior stole away with heaving shoulders, covering his face with his hands. His opponent, cock-a-hoop with victory, ran off in triumph down the street.

On another occasion when a ring formed outside the doctor's house, next door to Dean's, there was a dramatic interruption when the sister of one of the big-uns, who served as a maid, suddenly threw up a window on the upper floor and shouted to her brother 'Leave 'im go 'ome!' And to my surprise the ring broke up with only a brief protest. It didn't take me long to discover that taken by and large the village girls were far nicer than the boys.

I failed to evade the next challenge. Most boys and men are cowards at heart, and never, if they can help it, challenge anyone they aren't certain of beating, so when I was pushed into a ring with Jack, son of Tiny the genial proprietor of the Unicorn Inn, I knew I was in for a hiding. As usual the challenge was purely formal, merely an excuse for Jack to increase his reputation as a fighter. So he chose me, the town boy whom anyone could beat. Before I knew what had happened his fists were crashing into my undefended face, as I knew nothing of boxing. Neither did Jack, or indeed anyone at the school. A fight consisted of wading in until one was beaten. I was beaten well before I started, having been all day in a blue funk. Soon I had had enough and collapsed in a blubbering heap. I can see the contempt in Jack's eyes now, but I was soon to make amends. One day by sheer mischance I pricked the boy who was sitting in front with a compass needle. He at once flung round and told me there was going to be a fight that evening. The boy in question I had hitherto regarded as a friend, as we were neighbours. He had never proved aggressive before, but now he was telling everyone what he intended doing to me. I was then about ten and he a year or two older, a strong boy who could kick a football out of sight. For some reason his boastful threats didn't frighten me and I determined to give as good as I received. So when the ring formed without waiting I rushed in swinging at the face. From then on I never stopped until he dropped his arms and murmured 'Christ!' which was the signal that he'd had enough. I experienced such a feeling of elation that I felt for an instant like taking on the whole school. But the other boys were disappointed. A rank outsider had achieved the impossible by drubbing a villager and that wasn't allowed.

Congratulations, however, came from an unexpected quarter. As I ran down the street the joiner's wife, who had apparently been watching the contest, looked at me with admiration in her eyes and said 'You beat 'im didn't you?' My victory earned me one positive advantage, since I was no longer threatened with challences any more.

I had been till then a rabbit at football. Football was played on Wednesday afternoons on Tiny Jones's field, and Tiny, who was a football addict, usually came to watch and talk to Dean. Dean, I suspect, knew as little about football as I did, but liked people to think that he did. It was part of his image as the man who was boss of all he surveyed.

To begin with I didn't even know how to kick a football, never having been taught or shown how to play, so when I was put at centre-forward I had no idea what I was supposed to do. I was moved out on the wing, where I did a little better but remained for the rest of the season a figure of contempt.

The following year, an odd thing happened. Tiny who had been watching my vain flounderings suddenly suggested to Dean that I went in goal. Carpenter was the regular goalkeeper for the team, so his switching to an outside rôle in favour of myself caused some consternation. To everyone's surprise I proved a success and pushed a hard shot over the bar. 'I thought you was going to loose 'im through,' Ronnie Parsons, the head keeper's son, confided as we left the field. The comment thrilled me. For the first time in my life I was winning praise from a villager, and that was praise indeed. I began to feel at long last that I had actually arrived and could hold my head up in local society. In fact I joined the yobs' kick about in the Park Meadow on early spring evenings and received some encouragement from Curly Davies, the best footballer in the school. So football was OK. But birds were better.

10 Wild Boar Paste, Moorhens and Jackdaws

I had run into Manley's clutching a sixpenny bit and four coppers. I was wearing, I recall, a loose fitting dark green jumper which my mother had knitted, pulled down over a pair of grey shorts. Was it there? I scanned the neat rows of potted meat and fish arranged on the shelves behind the counter examining the labels. The assistant, a youth of two and twenty with a frank open face and laughing eyes, was busy attending to a tramplike character called Walter who lived with his aged wife in a tiny cottage down the Back Lane.

'Shan't last long, now,' the old man prophesied gloomily, as the assistant handed him a bottle of cough cure. The youth, who was called Tom, gave a look of mock outrage. 'Let's see,' he grinned, snatching the bottle back and gazing intently at the label as if it claimed that the contents were the elixir of life. 'As I thought, Walter. You've got the very stuff there. You'll soon be as right as rain.' The old man pocketed the bottle and edged away, growling in disbelief.

The assistant turned back to face me as I continued to quiz the pots. 'Well, young Pinkie, what be it this time? Veal and 'am or salmon and shrimp?' 'Wild boar, please Tom,' I piped. 'Wild boar?' The assistant's eyebrows knitted in perplexity. 'You've come to the wrong shop. We don't keep boar or polar bear if it comes to that.' 'There be always one, Tom,' I persisted. 'There, just be'ind your 'ead.' 'Bless me, if the kid bent right.' The youth reread the inscription to make sure. ' 'Ere it be. Same price as the others. What do it taste like?' 'Lovely,' I answered, clasping my prize. 'Thanks, Tom,' I added, running out through the door.

The assistant gazed after me, shaking his head. 'Odd kid that,' I heard him mutter. 'Bit of a loner and always getting scragged'. Wild boar paste. How was it he'd never noticed it before?

Out on the pavement I quickly engaged in a wild boar hunt. Swerving to the right and left to escape the lethal thrusts of the gleaming tushes I collided with the rotund figure of the police sergeant, posed majestically outside the entrance to the Red Lion.

'Eh out, young Pinkie!' the officer roared. 'Why don't you look where you be agoing? I've a good mind . . .'

But I was already out of earshot and darted like a rabbit making for its burrow into the passage behind the grocer's shop, which led, via the garden to the kitchen door. 'What on earth's the matter?' Nana looked up from the range where she was baking rock cakes. 'Look after this, please, Nana,' I panted. 'I'm just going up the garden.' 'Wild boar paste!' the lady repeated in contempt. 'His father and mother are too soft with that boy.'

Wild boar paste would do nicely for my supper, I argued as I raced along. And as for lunch, a moorhen's egg would be just the thing, washed down, of course, by a cup of Camp coffee. Moorhens' eggs were readily obtainable from the nest on the Bearcroft pool. I had only to open the door in the wall at the top of the garden, jump the stile in the hedge which bounded Hope's meadow and dart across the turf to the pool. The pool was quite small, forty or fifty yards long at the most, fringed with sallies on the nearer side and with brambles beyond. The nest lay in an awkward place, above the water, but I could just reach it by lying on my stomach above the bushes and groping with my hand. The bird scuttled off as my fingers dabbled gingerly among the obstructing thorns. 'Good! Three eggs.' I never took more than one in the secure knowledge that the bird could be relied upon to make up the complement next day. I looked round guiltily as I rose to my feet, just in case Mabel, the farmer's daughter, was watching. She had once popped out of nowhere when I'd crept up the orchard fence to steal an apple, fondly imagining I was unobserved. But Mabel's eyes were everywhere and the sharp lashing she had given me with her tongue had hurt far worse than a cut with her stick.

When I returned to the kitchen I was relieved to find that Nana had retired upstairs. Peering into the cupboard below the dresser my eyes lighted on the white basin which I always used. Extracting a hatpin from the spot where I'd hidden it behind the clock I carefully drilled the egg at either end before blowing the reddish fluid into the basin. Next I whipped it with a fork into a froth before transferring it into an aluminium saucepan. Adding a pat of butter and a pinch of salt I scrambled the contents expertly over the range till it was nice and crumbly and, the crowning touch, slightly black and burned. I always insisted on doing the scrambling myself for no mere female, not even Nana, could be trusted to scramble an egg properly, much less a moorhen's, without leaving it runny and underdone.

Next came the Camp coffee. Taking down the bottle from the larder shelf I measured out a teaspoonful of the black syrup into a cup while waiting for the milk to boil. Adding two teaspoonfuls of sugar I sipped the ambrosial concoction with the air of a connoisseur before setting the cup beside the egg. Gazing at the Scottish soldier portrayed on the label I wondered just how many soldiers there really were, for the soldier was holding a coffee bottle on a tray with a similar soldier holding an identical bottle . . .

Tom Price the sexton – it was odd the number of villagers I knew called Tom, not counting my father and brother – was busy digging the garden when I returned. He was a short bright-faced man, with eyes that twinkled like a ferret's under the peak of his cloth cap. 'Seen where I bin digging, Tom?' I pointed to the small patch of earth which I proudly termed my 'garden'. Removing his pipe the sexton spat and leant on his spade. 'Looks as though an 'al 'en a-bin scratchin' there', he commented uncharitably. 'When you comin' to see them jackdaws?'

'Oh can I, Tom?' Jackdaws, I knew, lived in the church tower and their nests got in Tom's way whenever he went to wind the clock. 'Be there any eggs yet, Tom?' 'Eggs? Ay, plenty. Chicks too. Too many of the dang things.' 'Oh, please, Tom, when can we go?' I pleaded. 'Tharternoon, if you likes, when I finished digging this 'ere patch for your dad'.

Half an hour later we crossed the churchyard and approached the door which led to the tower steps. The sexton drew a key from an inner pocket and undid the lock. In a recess at the bottom of the flight of stone stairs stood a light vehicle with wheels like a pram. 'What be that, Tom?' I inquired. 'Carries coffins,' the man answered shortly, picking up a large bath broom.

Ascending the steps we hadn't gone far when we found the way blocked by a pile of sticks. The sticks formed a cradle for the nest itself which was lined with sheep's wool and contained three eggs. The eggs were coloured blue and prettily decorated with little brown blotches and tiny black spots. 'Want 'em?' the sexton inquired, 'afore I sweeps 'em down.' 'Yes, please, Tom. But where shall I put 'em?' 'Ought to 'ave brought a tin.' my companion grumbled. 'Owsoever you can carry 'em careful like in your pocket arter you wrapped 'em in some o' this 'ere wool.'

I followed my mentor's bidding, stooping to retrieve the eggs. Meantime Tom pulled out a wad of wool before sweeping the nest down the stairway with a blow from the massive broom. Continuing our ascent we reached the big chamber where the ringers pulled the bells. The ropes hung down red and dusty, just out of my reach. 'P'raps you'll ring 'em one day,' the sexton prognosticated, 'when you've growed.' A second nest impeded our progress, but in place of eggs it contained two chicks, fully fledged and squawking hungrily. 'Want 'em?' the man repeated, raising his broom. 'If not I'll sweep 'em down.' 'Oh no! Don't sweep 'em down, Tom!' I begged. 'I'll look arter 'em. I'll keep 'em in the parrot's cage.' The parrot had come when my great uncle Walter died, but had soon followed its former owner. 'You'll 'a 'to feed 'em,' the sexton counselled, 'an' I don't mean once a day.' 'What shall I feed 'em on, Tom?' 'Lights,' the man barked succinctly. 'Lights from Jim's.'

Jim Basset was the genial butcher who kept greyhounds and went coursing on Sundays when others went to church. That was one problem solved, but I was wondering how I could manage to carry the young birds.

'Wait a bit. I've got a sack somewheres.' Tom had already anticipated difficulty. 'Ah – 'ere it be. Put 'em in that.'

I returned delighted with my protesting burden and ran up the steps to the shed's upper storey. Opening the cage I gently lifted the birds inside. They gaped and chirped unhappily, squatting at the bottom, a pair of miserable orphans waiting for their parents to bring them food, the parents they would never see.

I paused for a moment considering, then suddenly made up my mind. Jim's shop occupied a windy corner at the top of the street. Jim was a character. He paused in the act of chopping a leg of lamb with a half-humorous, half quizzical leer. 'Well, young Pinkie,' he greeted amiably, 'what be up with you?' 'Please, Jim.' I blurted, wriggling with embarrassment. 'Please will you give me some lights.' 'LIGHTS?' the butcher exploded. 'Why d'you want lights?' 'To feed my jackdaws.'

The man's jaw dropped in amazement. 'To feed your jackdaws,' he repeatedly uncomprehendingly. 'What in 'ell d'you want jackdaws for?' 'Got them from Tom, up in the church tower,' I explained, while the butcher continued chopping the bone. ''Ere you be!' he bellowed suddenly, delving under the bench. 'That do?' He held up a bloody mass of offal for my inspection. 'Oh, thank you, Jim,' I enthused. 'I'll just wrap 'em up in a bit of newspaper,' the butcher went on. Snatching the dripping parcel with a grin I scampered happily off home.

But moorhens and jackdaws were small fry in comparison with other birds I knew.

11 Bird's nesting, Workhouse and Gilbert Harding

The eerie bleat-like trill of a snipe drumming high in the air is one of the most exciting sounds I know. That and the plaintive cry of the peewit are indelibly associated with spring and the Park Meadow. The Park Meadow was the biggest tract of grass in the neighbourhood and measured a mile around. It stretched all the way from the churchyard to the Brook, which formed its long north western boundary and had formerly produced record crops of hay. At least so Al' Annie once told me. She and her brother Jim Hope owned the meadow, as well as its neighbour the Park Field, and lived at the Throne Farm. Then had come the sewage scheme and the great meadow was converted, almost overnight, into a wilderness of mud and marshes. There was still, it was true, sufficient grassland left for a football pitch, but the rest was waste, the haunt of peewits, snipe and curlew and even teal and redshank on occasion. In the opinion of a bird-crazy boy the sewage scheme brought nothing but benefit. The sewage was collected from the village in a reservoir, covered by a shed known as the Jam Factory. It was then distributed in a series of ditches which criss-crossed the meadow right down to the Brook. They were filled to overflowing with black evil-smelling ordure, which popular though it was with peewits and curlews, made me unpopular with the family when carried into the house on my boots and deposited on the carpet.

Bird's-nesting is a reprehensible activity, but in those days you would have found few boys to agree with you. Besides, peewits' nests in the Park Meadow were two a penny. I once found a nest which had been drowned in a puddle. So I placed all four eggs in an adjacent nest and when I returned a day or two later the peewit was brooding all eight. So bird's-nesting wasn't all bad. When I grew older I used a box camera to take shots of curlews' and peewits' nests, but in the meantime, like everyone else, I started to make an egg collection. Even then taking eggs was forbidden by law and there was a long list of protected species pasted on the notice board outside the police station. The police were on watch, and Jim and I were once challenged by the local bobby when crossing Dent's meadow. But Jim talked him out of it. Jim was my pal. His father was a builder and he was the most generous soul alive. His sister Nancy kept a shop in the Back Lane and on our excursions Jim would share a cake, or any other welcome titbit which he happened to have brought along. Jim was a year or two older than I was and remained my close friend till he bought a brown trilby and joined the yobs on the corner at the top of the street.

Hedgers and ditchers are now thin on the ground. Not so seventy years ago when retired farm labourers were often so employed. Jim and I were bird's-nesting when a sound like an enraged badger attracted our attention. At first we were puzzled till a white bearded face, feebly waving a stick and mouthing obscenities, appeared through a gap in the hedge.

'It be Al' Murrell!' Jim laughed in relief. Murrell was the oldest resident in the village.

Much worse than police were landowners like Al' Dent whose fields we often trespassed on. Al' was employed in a double sense. In the first place it described people you feared and, in the second, those you didn't. Modern parallels would be Al' 'itler and Al 'Monty, as referred to by troops during the war.

One day Tommy, my six year old brother, and I joined a crowd of boys aiming to cross the brook by a fallen tree and visit Dent's fields. At first all went well until Sid, the big-un who was leading us, noticed a motorcar stopping by the road.

''Eh out!' he warned. 'It be Al' Dent.'

Dent's car was a village joke, because he always drove it in bottom gear, but it wasn't so funny watching him getting out. Sid told us to lie down and keep silent, but it was clear that we'd been spotted and Dent had a short way with trespassers. Climbing over a gate he advanced towards us, whip in hand. In the end one of the boys lost his nerve and ran back towards the Brook. It was a signal for a general exodus and in no time at all we were scrambling over the tree. All except one. Where was Tommy? He had lost his way and was running up and down the bank like a cornered chicken.

'Jump, Tommy! Jump!', we chorused as Dent's shouts came nearer and nearer. In the end he did just that, only to land in midstream and emerge covered in filth.

I didn't visit only the Park Meadow and its immediate surroundings in search of birds' nests. Search as I would I couldn't find a curlew's until someone suggested the Boggy Pool. To get to the pool you turned off at the bottom of the Folly Lane, a high-hedged trackway which led to a big farm house called The Homme. The Homme belonged to the Pudges, who owned the field where the pool was situated, and it was all new territory to me. However, I managed to persuade my father one Whit Monday, a good time for curlews, to accompany me on this expedition into the unknown. In due course we entered the field and had hardly begun to cross it when a large bird rose at our feet. There was the nest, containing three eggs, lying in a scrape among some rushes. Curlew's eggs are big, as big as turkey's and I was naturally delighted by my success.

A great love of mine was turtle doves, those lovely small mauve coloured pigeons which appeared each year in May. I could never find a nest, even though one bird came down to feed with the fowls. Then one day while my brother and I were roaming about Hope's meadow we crossed over from the Bearcroft into the orchard beyond, which was filled with cider apple trees. In those days most farmers made their own cider. In the farmyards was usually found the press, an immense wood and iron instrument to squeeze out the juice of apples and pears. The juice was left to mature in casks and whenever you called on a farmer he would offer you a sample or two and invite your opinion. Chancing to glance upwards I noticed a platform of frail sticks far finer than those of a wood pigeon. My heart beat faster. Surely it must be? Or was it? For some reason I suggested my brother climb the tree whilst I waited expectantly below. Before long a bird came tumbling down from the nest and proceeded to roll about on the grass, attempting in vain to distract our attention.

'Any eggs?', I shouted in breathless excitement. 'Yes, two', my brother's voice came down from the sky. 'How big?' 'Size of a blackbird's'. On hearing this I rolled like the dove on the ground in ecstasy for I'd found a turtle dove's nest at last.

'They're sacred birds', Johnny Davies reminded me when I met him later. 'They be mentioned in the Bible. You best let them alone'. Johnny was curiously well informed and he and I often discussed subjects like heaven and death. 'What a day it will be', he once observed as we strolled searching for long-tailed tits' nests in the hawthorns beside the Brook, 'when the dead meet in heaven'.

My interest in birds was by no means confined to bird's-nesting. I also kept birds from time to time, like the ill-fated jackdaws. Aware of my interests, a local man once arrived in the shop with a basket containing three young barn owls. As the birds were only partially fledged it was clear that their feeding would prove even more difficult than the daws', so having ascertained from the man the location of the nest I decided to take them back the following day. In the meantime I took them to my bedroom and put them underneath a towel before going to sleep. The rest of the family, as well as the Manleys, were kept awake by the sound of the parent owls screeching round the windows all night. It was an incredible performance on their part since the nest lay several miles away. How they managed to locate the nestlings I cannot imagine. Certainly I never even glimpsed their presence when I returned the young birds to the top of a willow tree, where the nest was surrounded with dead mice. But my interest in keeping birds withered with age. Young carrion crows went the way of the jackdaws, while the pigeons flew home. I did keep a pair of young little owls, known as French or Partridge owls by the locals, but Nana let them out.

Weobley in winter.

A path through the Park Meadow led to the local poor law institution, known as the workhouse, with which we were soon destined to become acquainted.

The Dickensian image of workhouses was not entirely ill-founded, and their disappearance after World War II was a good thing. They had served a useful purpose when the poor received no benefits from the state and, if they lost their living, went hungry. Poverty has always been regarded as a social stigma and to be incarcerated in a workhouse the most abject fate of all, for inmates, for the most part, were treated like servants, while the masters and their families were revered like lords. Gilbert Harding, the former television personality, who was born at Hereford workhouse, describes in his autobiography *Along My Line* how corrupting it was to be called Master Gilbert and to have a mother who never worked, as later on you discovered that it all counted for nothing and that you tended to be looked down on. So it was hardly surprising that as friends of Leonard, the master's son, Tom and I thoroughly enjoyed our visits to Weobley workhouse, which, from our privileged point of view, was a place of space and leisure where we spent some of the happiest days of our lives.

In the Fosters' time the workhouse was always half empty. So much so indeed that we came to know most of the inmates, like the starchy Jane Wall who assisted in the kitchen and old decrepit Jane Chip with a joke and a twinkling eye. There was also half-witted old Billy, clad in ill-fitting corduroys, whose sole function in life was to fetch the daily paper.

You entered the building, which was made of red brick and dated from 1837, through a lodge, where tramps were registered, and passed through the kitchen before proceeding upstairs. The kitchen smelt of stale meat and carbolic soap, as did the refectory, where the men, women and occasional children sat on rough benches and ate off deal tables which were always scrubbed clean. Scrubbing occupied the women for much of their time, while the men dug the large patch of garden or sometimes cracked stones.

The porter, Sidney, was the master's brother. He took his meals with the family and retreated to his cubbyhole in the lodge when he had nothing better to do. He was a small man with a fierce moustache, twisted into points at the ends, and invariably wore an old russet coloured suit. He was generally friendly, but could adopt an appropriately fierce attitude whenever a casual, as tramps were known, chanced to turn up. When feeling sportive we would call him Doncaster, an asinine sounding sobriquet which never failed to rouse him. Presumably he had once lived in that northern town. The result would be a chase, ending in boxed ears. For all that, we loved him and in more sober moments he would take down the single barrelled muzzle-loader, which was his pride and joy, and put it to his shoulder. 'She comes up lovely!' he would croon. 'Did I ever tell you about the 'are? I didn't notice the old bloke till after I'd fired and 'e lets out a 'ell of a yell.'

The person we loved most among the workhouse staff was Nurse Johnson. An elderly woman with grey hair and bun, she came of Welsh border farming stock and loved boys above all creatures. She delighted to entertain us in her room where she'd open tins of fruit and tell us tales of coursing hares on her father's farm. She had been at the workhouse during the war, when it was used to accommodate prisoners.

'They weren't bad fellows,' she'd remark reminiscently of the Poles, as she poured out a glass of lemonade. She was a mine of gossip where the village was concerned and when we left posted us a complete budget of local news. She used to lend me books of an ancient and highly curious character. One, I remember, was called simply *Queer Tales*. And they were, including as they did pig-faced women.

One Sunday she accompanied us, as she often did, pushing Leonard's infant brother in the pram to Sarnesfield, a tiny hamlet graced with a 'court'. A little further on the road was joined by another and beyond loomed the outline of the Black Mountains. This was enough for me. 'We'll walk to Abergavenny!' I announced boldly. 'It isn't really very far.'

It was in fact the better part of forty miles but Leonard and my young brother didn't know that. I encouraged them with imaginary descriptions of the welcome we should receive by my aunts and cousins and soon their enthusiasm began to match mine. Alas, in the end little Tommy began to feel tired and when we reached a sign-post stating that Weobley was still three miles away he finally broke down moaning 'Oh dear! Oh dear!' At that point my plans collapsed and an extremely weary and disillusioned three small boys struggled up the hill for home. Meantime a hue and cry had been raised, not least by Nurse Johnson. She did little to cheer either parents by claiming she had heard shouts and screams coming from the region of the Brook. At long last we toiled up the village street, while Leonard ran off to face the music. It was an extraordinary adventure which could have ended in disaster, and all due to the vivid and heated imagination which I had inherited from my father.

As for the Fosters' private apartments in addition to a dining room there was a big comfortable lounge, furnished with four windows, each of which commanded a view of the yards. The yards were designed to keep the sexes separate and this included the girls and boys. One day Bumper and his sisters were taken into care and greeted us as old friends. The lounge was as nothing in comparison with the grand board room where the Guardians gathered from time to time. The Guardians consisted of the local gentry, whose stately limousines lined the drive for all the world like a royal visitation. We were rarely admitted to its awful precincts. When we did the much polished table reflected our faces like glass. It was a highly autocratic régime, though we were hardly aware of it at the time. Like Gilbert, Leonard was respectfully addressed by the inmates with the prefix 'master', which we found somewhat strange. But he was skilled in such practical arts as skinning rabbits and setting mole traps which quickly won our admiration: he is still my oldest friend. What we enjoyed most was scampering round the lawns up and down the long through-drive with gates at either end, all maintained in immaculate order, or running through the immense vegetable plot down to the brook. At other times we rabbited with Jim, the Irish terrier, in the adjacent fields, for in those days the world was our oyster and we wandered wherever we chose. There was also the Drying Field, where they hung out the washing, with a stream to make mud pies.

When the weather was wet we would play in one of the empty bedrooms or retire to the lounge and Leonard's toys. Sometimes, in the evening, Mr Foster, who had served in the cavalry during the Boer War, would spread cushions round the floor and play war games based on his experiences in South Africa. At other times, when the weather was fine, he'd help us build a fort, from which we launched clay cannon balls through a drainpipe at uncle Sid. The fort became a kind of second home, where we kept even a collection of birds' eggs. Philip Foster was a tall, fine looking man with a clipped moustache and soldierly bearing, who took us fishing, *pace* the Guardians, for perch in nearby Sarnesfield pool and from a punt at Letton. His wife Ellen was a superior lady and a firm disciplinarian on occasion.

It was through the Fosters that we met Gilbert Harding and his grandfather, who took over the Hereford workhouse when Gilbert's father died. Grandfather was a trim, priggish man with a white beard, who cycled over to visit the Fosters. At other times Gilbert's sister Connie came to stay. Connie was a big rumbustious lass of twenty with a loud irreverent chuckle and a cannonball tennis service which rarely went in. Unlike her brother she liked small boys and everybody loved her. The irascible Gilbert became a byword for outspoken comment on the popular television programme 'What's my line'? Unlike other entertainers he never minded what he said. And what he said was generally true. After a mixed career, in which he became friendly with G.K. Chesterton and served his time as a teacher and a policeman, he found his métier in broadcasting during World War II and subsequently on television.

One morning he arrived outside our house, accompanied by Leonard. He was then I suppose in his late teens and had just started at Cambridge. When we met him he was engaged in an altercation with Leonard. What Leonard had done to annoy him wasn't clear, but if we'd expected another Connie we were in for a disappointment. At a loss to entertain him we suggested that he might like to take the country path back to the workhouse via the Park Meadow. Gilbert, unfortunately, was hardly dressed suitably for a rustic ramble. His beautifully creased suit and grey spats would not have excited comment on King's Parade, but were hardly in place in a field full of sewage.

We inquired whether he might care to see a wren's nest, which, in the vernacular, we happened to 'know to', and he at once agreed. The nest was in a sally tree, as willows were called, and contained, since wrens are prodigal in this respect, a round dozen eggs. Gilbert wished to see one, so I carefully extracted a tiny pink globe and laid it on his palm. He was simply delighted and asked if he could keep it. Relieved to have pleased him we all agreed, and after wrapping the egg in a handkerchief he put it in his pocket.

Just then someone mentioned the Jam Factory. Gilbert's eyebrows shot up in surprise till we explained what it really was. Then an unfortunate thing happened. Gilbert, unthinking, clapped a hand to his pocket and broke the egg. The next moment a mucous fluid oozed through the lining and the air became blue.

I never met Gilbert Harding again. On television his tantrums amused the public and he was dubbed the common man's philosopher. He might have earned fame as a barrister had he exercised more discipline and succeeded in controlling his temper, in which case television audiences would have been denied a good deal of entertainment when listening to his flights of hard commonsense.

A notable annual event at the workhouse was Bonfire Night when the Fosters and their friends gathered round an enormous pile of wood with Guy Fawkes himself, with a mangel wurzel head, propped up aloft ready to be burned. We boys accumulated a store of fireworks well in advance, and when the fire was lit and rockets brightened the November sky we were often guilty, I regret to say, of attaching jack-jumpers to the coat-tails of innocent bystanders.

12 Choral society, Parties, Plays and Fêtes

Weobley was a democracy in which everybody shared: everyone knew everyone else and tended to do the same things. Everything happened within walking distance, whether a cinema show, a fancy dress party, a play, a garden fête or a meeting of the Choral Society. The Choral Society was very popular, especially among the women. Anyone with the least pretensions as a singer was welcome and at the annual public performance there were frequently as many in the chorus on the stage as in the actual audience.

My mother and father were members of the Choral Society, my mother as a singer and my father as a member of the orchestra, in which he played the violin. The orchestra was led by the remarkable Stanley Tait, a violinist of professional rank. Raised in Newcastle, his father had wasted his substance on travel and ended up as a grocer in Weobley. Stanley was a flower which bloomed unseen, content with his pupils and the local musical talent. His brothers Arthur and Gardner took part also, playing the cello and viola respectively. But they weren't in the same class as Stanley. Arthur in particular, who was not only responsible for the bakery side of the business but acted as a motor mechanic as well, found the going hard. Gardner, on the other hand, was a card and the only one of the three eventually to get married. Later my father ran an orchestra of his own, and was invited by the Verdins to perform at Garnstone Castle.

The chorus was trained by a man named Proctor who travelled over from Hereford. Proctor was a character and a lively and efficient director who got the most out of the class. So, when the great day came, the village was regaled with excerpts from *Faust, Merry England, Tom Jones* and *Maritana*.

Children's fancy dress parties were held annually in the Recreation Hall, a black and white building on the Kington Road which had originally served as a tithe barn. As ancient Egypt was constantly in the news, through the discoveries associated with Tut-ankh-amun, I decided to go as Rameses the Second. Why not Tut-ankh-amun himself I cannot remember. Perhaps I possessed a suitable picture of the former monarch, though Tut in his glory was always being figured. At any rate my choice stimulated considerable interest and my neighbour, Mrs Manley, proved an expert on detail. So I was provided with a head–dress, uraeus and sandals and was firmly convinced that I would be awarded first prize. But the judge, the Reverend Mr. Marshall, who owned the Sarnesfield estate, thought otherwise and I was placed second after a girl disguised as a chocolate box.

The prizegiving was followed by dancing. For the only time in my life I took part in the lancers partnered by Ellen Foster, but the favourite was Roger de Coverley.

Plays were performed in the Recreation Hall by itinerant bands of actors. They were usually old favourites like *Maria Martin*, who was murdered by her lover William Cawdor in the Red Barn back in the eighteenth century. The high point in the version presented at Weobley was when Cawdor chased his victim round the stage waving, of all things, a rifle. After he'd fired the fatal shot the result was revealed by a red blob of ink on Maria's temple. As she fell he caught her in his arms uttering the moving words 'I loved her. Yes I did!'

Equally dramatic was *Lady Audley's Secret*. The heroine, an immense elderly woman with a presence and voice like Wilde's Lady Bracknell, got rid of her husband by pushing him down a well, only he didn't fall down the well at all and in the last scene reappeared. The sight proved too much for Lady Audley who shrieked and collapsed in her lover's arms, whereupon the latter, gazing sorrowfully into her eyes, murmured like Cawdor (being of course the same actor), 'The soul still lingers, but the mind has flown.'

In lighter vein was *Charlie's Aunt*, when the elderly lover caused much amusement by his addresses to the man in disguise. 'I see you!' he crooned, as he admired the supposed lady, while the latter muttered sotto voce 'Old fool!'

There was a play which featured a man (acted by the oldest member of the cast) who had been prevented by his mother from ever setting eyes on a girl. Instead he was sent to play with the ducks and wandered quack quacking up and down the stage. Inevitably he eventually met a girl, exclaiming 'What a pretty bird!' How the play ended I do not remember, but it provided many a laugh.

Even more absurd was the story of a man who had received an invitation from his brother who lived in the country saying 'Dear brother Bill, come down and enjoy yourself'. The house unfortunately contained a ghost, dressed in a white sheet, which kept running across the stage until shot dead. None of this was quite Hamlet or Irving, but nobody cared about that.

Other entertainments were sometimes provided when members of the audience were invited to take part. One evening the sportive Fred Hope was invited to enter the tent of a female fortune teller only to emerge with a bucket on his head, while an inebriated chauffeur went quite mad and cavorted about like a dervish. Old soldiers were cajoled to sing barrack-room songs to the general scandal, but such behaviour was the exception and the entertainment provided by the actors was always properly conducted. My mother sang and acted too in amateur dramatics.

The author in fancy dress.

Other popular events were whist drives and dances in which I took no part, but I did attend dancing classes from the age of nine held in the former Drill Hall. The dances were conducted by a plain active woman in her thirties who taught us the polka and waltz. I enjoyed the sessions at such a young age, but when I grew older I was too shy to take part. Other pupils from Weobley school attended, spruced up, if boys, in clean jerseys, while the girls wore party frocks. At such times, even the big-un who had screwed my ear would growl confidingly, 'You wants to be in class one upper, Polly. Don't us 'ave some fun!' The precise nature of the fun I never knew, though it was probably in Dean's absence after his wife's death.

'I got somethin' better'n your al' bike,' he announced on another occasion. 'I gotta 'norse.' I had recently acquired a secondhand Raleigh and my schoolmates were predictably jealous, indeed so much so that they would form a chain across the road to prevent me riding by.

Fêtes were held in summer at suitable sites both in the village and elsewhere. One at Lloyds 'The Field', a farm on the outskirts opposite Garnstone, offered as an attraction real ice cream. It was run by three spinster sisters, one of whom, Milly, became a friend. Apart from the ices the thing I remember most was finding a stock-dove's nest in a hole in a tree. Most convenient was the fête held by the Manleys next door to our house. One of the items was a ladies' ankle competition, in which the contestants' identity was hidden by a blanket. Jim Basset was elected judge, but his wife's blue skirt projected and he commented amid laughter, 'I've had an opportunity of admiring those before.' In the end he diplomatically awarded the prize to a total stranger, not without charm herself.

There were also tennis parties, but these tended to be private affairs. There were tournaments too in which players from other places were invited to compete. My father possessed a powerful service, but rarely did well when partnered by my mother, who was jealous of his expertise. We mostly played at Manleys along with their Quaker friends, and it was there that we made the acquaintance of two public school products, named Jack and Linley, who repelled us at first by their supercilious manners, but when they thawed later we became good friends.

'The Fair's come!' A posse of excited children freed from school ran down the hill to see if it were true. 'No it a'nt! No it a'nt!' a plump girl contradicted, unwilling to find her hopes dashed. ''An it 'as!' she shrieked in ecstasy as the fair came in view.

The May Fair was a major social event in Weobley, but of course it didn't compare with Hereford's in scale or variety. There was only a single round-about, consisting of galloping horses, but when this attracted business to the Red Lion in Broad Street, Tiny Jones engaged a fair of his own. In the end

The author's parents seated centre and right in a Weobley tennis party.

there were two fairs, one by the Tank and the other at the top of the village. Both seemed to thrive, but when gambling machines appeared they tended to divert interest from the traditional sideshows.

The popular songs of the moment, blaring forth from the roundabout organ, were 'Why did I kiss that Girl' and 'Chillibong bong'. There was also an amalgam of Highland reels called 'The Piper's Wedding' which set everbody's feet a-tapping. What happened to fair organs? I have often wondered. None have appeared on the Antiques Road Show. They were made in France and were examples of baroque art in their own right. As for the great traction engines, they were nowhere in view, Peters, the fairman, employing a gilded Foden steam waggon to draw his trucks. Like its big brothers it sported a dynamo too. Someone told me you could obtain free rides on the roundabout if you helped put it up, so I spent several hours happily guiding the iron pins, projecting from the wooden horses, into slots in the platform. In return I received a single grubby ticket. At least I had assisted in building the machine.

Only one circus visited Weobley in my time and that was Tom Fosset's. He erected his marquee in Tiny's field and captivated the villagers with a baby elephant. He gave pony rides inside the tent to the great delight of my sisters.

But what I remember best was an act by two clowns. One dressed as a professor sat on a chair, while the other took the part of his pupil wearing a dunce's hat. The professor then commenced to lecture on the history of the world, beginning with Adam and Eve.

'Adam came first and Eve came after,' he commenced portentously. 'And she's been after him ever since,' the other interjected as the professor knocked his hat off. Every time he ran off the latter recalled him with the comical reprimand 'Rabbit, caaaaaame here!' 'Rabbit, come here!' would have sounded quite flat, but using the past tense fairly brought the house down.

The wireless came to Weobley in my time there. Dean the schoolmaster was the first to possess a set, followed by the Taits and my father. The Taits knew a man who made wireless sets and ours was a splendid four valve receiver in a plain wooden case with the valves and coils mounted on top. It was powered by accumulators, which had to be taken to the Taits to be recharged from time to time. One of the valves had a red top and when my father was tuning the set a crimson glow illuminated his face. This feature didn't go unremarked so when he invited some beldams to listen to the radio for the very first time in their lives they half suspected that he was in league with Al' Nick.

The broadcasting stations in those days were Chelmsford and Daventry. We listened to the Children's Hour and the voices of 'uncles' and 'aunties', but never listened to programmes as a regular practice. There were too many other interesting things to do.

Very occasionally on summer nights, when we found it too hot to sleep, my brother and I would be invited by my parents to listen to Carrol Gibbons playing at the Savoy, but we were far too young to appreciate jazz, lacking as we did any sense of rhythm. Other famous broadcasts stick in the memory: the rolling periods of Ramsay Macdonald, when he became, in 1924, the first Labour prime minister; the opening of the Empire Exhibition at Wembley by King George V; Stanley Baldwin's reassuring words during the General Strike. And, of course, there was the News. Till then the world had relied on newspaper reports, which at best were one day old. Now it was possible to hear the news directly after something happened. Few people of our acquaintance listened to the News, preferring lighter programmes, but the information was there for those that wanted it.

Some saw the wireless as a rival, notably the vicar's wife. When services were broadcast she rightly foresaw that they could become an excuse for not going to church.

One morning as I was getting up I heard my father scream. My mother had reported that the set was on fire and he had seized the aerial lead. We boasted the highest aerial in the village, suspended from a pine pole. During the night the wind had blown it down across the electric cable. My mother saved my father's life by calmly taking the wire out of his hand. She was wearing plimsolls, the rubber soles of which are non-conducting, otherwise we should have all been orphaned.

The country itself offered relaxation during the autumn, as well as during the summer. Haymaking was then a communal pastime.

'They 'elps to lighten it,' a farmer explained when my brother and I strove to wield the pikles. At harvest time too it was exciting to watch the binder cutting swathes through the corn, or, later in the year, the threshing machine at work, belt-driven by a traction engine. Then there was the cider and perry making at the various farms. There was always plenty to watch and learn in the country.

A village is first and foremost a community. Weobley had its characters, men and women, and though they were never famous they shouldn't be forgotten. Most weren't my friends, since I was only a boy, but they all influenced my life.

13 Village Characters – the Men

Of all the interesting characters who lived in the village Tom Pugh shall have first place. He was the village coachman, old Tony Weller come to life. Every day he drove his horse brake to meet the train at Moorhampton station to return with boxes of merchandise for my father, or the occasional passenger. Tom was shortish and broad-shouldered with what is termed a weatherbeaten face, which he shaded with a curious slouch hat. He lived in a farm below the Nap with his two bachelor brothers and spinster sisters. The Nap was a modest eminence, crowned with a small field, where we sometimes picnicked. One brother, John, cut up logs for a living, while the younger brother Fred ran the farm. The two sisters, Lucy and Amelia, rarely emerged except at fair time, when they never walked further than the corner of the road. In the hall was a cabinet containing stuffed birds including a pink hawfinch killed with a stone while drinking in the stream behind the church.

In the stable yard at the back languished a motor car of early vintage. It was red, with brass lamps, and mudguards turned up at the ends. Tom had bought it to be in the fashion, but one outing was enough and he had returned to the horse.

His sole relaxation was to stroll up to the Red Lion of an evening and regularly present the same riddle: 'Well, mister,' he'd say, 'what be the two scarcest things in the world?'

Everyone present would assume a look of mystification while Tom chortled deep in his throat. 'Give up then, mister?' His eyes would twinkle and range round the faces. 'Why the sun and the moon, 'cos there be only one sun and only one moon. Quite right, mister?' On receipt of this information everyone would praise Tom's remarkable sagacity.

Tom kept an outsize brake for parties, which we would sometimes hire for jaunts. On such occasions I would always share the box and listen to his accounts of people and places. His boast was that he had never slept in a bed outside Weobley, though he had dossed down in his vehicle after hunt balls. He spoke with an adenoidal accent which, at times, was hard to interpret. 'Big hown over thar,' he would intone, 'belong to Majon Davey. Fine plane it be.'

Later I would get him on birds, but his range didn't extend much further than partridges and pheasants. 'Partridges be good al' English birds!' he said. 'Pheasants be var'ners.' 'There's a rook' I interrupted, 'or may be a carrion crow.' 'Don't like them carron crows,' he commented, mispronouncing the word. 'Grean blan thieves they be.'

There are no Toms now, nor horse brakes either, more's the pity.

I suppose the vicar should come next. The Reverend Leonard Edwards was in his sixties and lived by the church. The vicarage was a big white building, equipped with a tennis lawn where we sometimes played. Most days the vicar, who was tall and clean shaven with a clerical cast of countenance, would emerge and stride up through the village to call on the sick. His loud 'Good afternoon!' gave warning of his approach and the possibility that he might drop in for tea. He was a sportsman in a minor way, who sometimes took guests to shoot rabbits, and when we had snow he would accompany us to Garnstone Hill and join us in a ride on our toboggan.

Mrs Edwards was, in contrast to her mild-mannered husband, a woman of considerable presence. They had a daughter Hannah who bred spaniels, to the peril of callers' ankles. She also played the violin, tutored by Stanley Tait.

When the 'deah Bishop' (of Hereford) came, Mrs Edwards was in her element. The Right Reverend Linton Smith was a formidable character, physically strong and bullet-headed. He had rowed for his college at Oxford and been awarded a DSO for his service as a chaplain during World War I. He had come to Weobley as part of a pilgrimage which he was making round the diocese on foot. As far as I can remember he never spoke a word in public, though he appeared at an open air meeting as well as in church. Bishops in those days were treated like royalty and great things were hoped for after their visits. Mrs Edwards probably hoped for promotion for her husband, or at least a transfer, but nothing happened. It is hard to evaluate a man like Linton Smith. How, you wondered, did he regard himself? As a member of the church militant? Hardly. As a meek Christian priest? The notion is derisory. As one who kept his house in order? Certainly. The army had taught him the value of discipline and this he practised on the clergy with notable success. He was eventually translated to Rochester (bishops don't apply for jobs like ordinary mortals).

During the nineteen twenties there was no shortage of policemen. Even Weobley boasted a sergeant, as well as a constable, with the result that there was little crime. Only one murder had been committed in the district within living memory and that was some fifty years previously. Tiny Jones had pointed out the distant murder field with all due solemnity shortly after we arrived. A body had been found and the killer found, though nobody recalled the details. Murder, in those days, unlike today, was the rarest of crimes. Since the police knew everyone and everyone respected the police, offences in the major sense were virtually unknown. This was long before the days of carborne officers flashing their blue lamps. Sergeant Yapp and his colleague Hales patrolled the streets on foot, or, if summoned further afield, on pushbikes.

Sergeant Yapp in his fifties was a big impressive man, with a greying moustache and a well-fed stomach. His glance of disapproval, which closely resembled that of Kitchener on the poster, was calculated to make offenders quail. His measured tread, as he moved majestically along, made even the street corner boys, gathered outside Jim's shop, lower their voices and move out of his way. When they filled tins with carbide on Guy Fawkes night and exploded them with matches the sergeant reacted firmly in the belief that it was gunpowder. But he rarely made an arrest, since a word of warning was usually sufficient in such a closed society.

How many drovers, I wonder, survive to-day? Jack the drover was a familiar figure when he passed by the village herding cattle. He was long and lean with a yellow moustache, and aged I suppose about forty. He didn't just walk behind a herd, but doubled about like a sheepdog emitting piercing whistles to cut off strays. Since he was always on the move he rarely had time for conversation, apart from brief words with farmers who wanted their cattle moved. To drive sportive young bullocks past lane-ends and open gateways demands a degree of condition of which an athlete would be proud.

But even Jack was fallible. On one occasion when he was driving a herd of steers up the Back Lane, so avoiding the village, a beast broke rank and hared up the hill into Broad Street. The result was mayhem. Everyone ran for their lives, some even leaping the wall of Al' Griffiths's orchard beside the road. For a full half-hour a wild west rodeo took place in the main thoroughfare, with only Gregg, the grocer and revered JP, standing his ground and gallantly flapping a white apron in the recalcitrant beast's face. In the end Jack regained control, though considerably flustered by this temporary blow to his reputation.

I have wondered since what the farmers paid him. Did he receive a fixed sum per head or a lump sum for the entire herd? Probably he never got his due deserts any more than the blackberry pickers, who were lucky if they received a half-penny a pound from the local entrepreneur. He doubtless drove a hard bargain, but then he was unlikely to be paid much in excess of a penny a pound himself, after pushing the fruit in his handcart all the way to Hereford market.

Whatever Jack's financial circumstances at least he enjoyed local fame. It was grand to be known not as Jack Smith or Jack anybody else, but lordly Jack the drover. For other surname he apparently had none. At least I never heard it. Whether he was married I do not know. It was somehow impossible to imagine him settled anywhere. Like Puck he was ever on the move. Though a genial character for the most part he was probably not a man to cross.

Weobley was reputed to have been the original home of the famous white-faced breed of cattle. A man named Tomkins, who lived during the eighteenth century, was said to have been the originator of the Herefords we

Broad Street, Weobley.

know today. Tomkins had a second title to fame in that he fathered twenty-three children.

In those days stallions were walked from village to village to serve the mares. The walker I remember was small and dark and put up with his charge in the black and white building behind the Red Lion hotel, later claimed to be the oldest in England.

Al' Langford lived on a farm near the Marsh where he brewed cider. He was as round as one of his barrels and could be found on Sundays, surrounded by his cronies, sampling the various brews. The trouble was that he generously insisted on your sampling them too, to help you decide which you wanted to buy. Rough or farmhouse cider is a potent liquor which can rob a man of his legs. The cost of a firkin was two and sixpence, laughable by contemporary standards, but then those were the days when a large loaf of bread cost eightpence and a small half that amount. Eggs were a shilling a dozen and bananas thirteen a shilling. In those days people's expectations were low and few went away on holiday. Apart from soldiers or sailors, few had ever been abroad. To make a living was all most people could ask, and the privilege of enjoying local amusements like the mobile cinema, football, cricket, fêtes and the fair.

Al' Billy, William Verdin, was the local squire. On Sundays he and his wife were driven to church in a khaki coloured Armstrong-Siddeley car and sat motionless in a special railed off section. When the service was over, of which, being deaf, he heard nothing, the tiny pair would walk arm in arm up Broad Street, pass through the castle ruins and so return to Garnstone. On one occasion my parents and we children were passing the east lodge when we met Mrs. Verdin, an affable lady. The Verdins employed half the village whether as gamekeepers, gardeners, woodmen or domestics. Pheasants were raised on the estate in impressive numbers for the squire and his guests to shoot.

Once a year the grounds of Garnstone Castle were opened to the public, when Gilbert, the head gardener, showed everybody round. Gardeners of large estates can be proprietorial and testy, but everyone loved Gilbert with his two good looking daughters, pleasant wife and pet cats. But he was doomed to die young, not long after Al' Billy, whose last days had been darkened by the death of his only daughter who ran the girl guides. Alas, nothing remains now of the house as it was demolished in 1959.

Mr Norman lived in a little square house at the top of White Hill with his good looking wife and large family. He was short and dark with a matching beard and never missed chapel on Sunday. What he did for a living wasn't always clear, since he appeared to have a finger in several pies. But whatever he did in his modest way always seemed to prosper. He was the model of a happy man with a quiverful of children who ranged in age from two years to twenty. Whenever he returned from chapel, pushing his bike, the hedges re-echoed to the sound of hymns.

Like his wife, all his daughters were beautiful. The eldest and youngest were fair like their mother, while Margaret was as dark as night. She always wore a kilt at school, which pleased an itinerant bag-piper when he paid the village a visit. He was in the full dress of a Highland regiment and despite Dean's derogatory remarks the children followed him about like his Hamelin name-sake. Margaret was invariably top of the class.

Her father would do anything for you. On the rare occasions he visited Hereford you could give him a list of purchases and be sure he'd return with them all. He was a practising Christian, who put into effect the teachings of the Bible.

Then there was Bummer. Plays and concerts were rarely conducted without rude interruptions from the boys at the back. The seats were raised in tiers at the end of the hall facing the stage and on the topmost flights would assemble the youthful troublemakers. Normally they congregated on the corner at the top of the street, but when anything more exciting was in view they swiftly made their presence known to the general annoyance of those who had come to watch.

'I really think we ought to do something for these boys', the vicar once remarked to my father. My father agreed, recalling that I had recently received a game of Blow Football as a present. Blow Football is played on a table with a ping pong ball and paper pipes. It does very well to entertain small children, but is unlikely to excite the interest of teenage youths. Undeterred, my father and the vicar duly invited the youths to gather at the Recreation Hall in the hope of persuading them to indulge in a quiet evening's fun instead of worrying the police.

Bummer was the leader of this youthful gang. To say that he was lively is vastly to understate the case since nobody could forecast what Bummer would get up to especially after he took to riding a pennyfarthing cycle around the village. Where he had acquired it nobody knew, but he rode it with all the skill of a Victorian racer. Arrived at a gathering he would make his presence known by bellowing witticisms in a foghorn-like voice. The other youths took their cue from him and it all usually ended in uproar. The well meant attempt to introduce Blow Football met the same fate. After a few minutes blowing the ball around the youths grew bored and began to misbehave. Defeated, my father and the vicar left the hall crouching low under a shower of apple cores.

Equally memorable, but very different, was Ernie Hill. Ernie's whistling was the loudest and most musical I ever heard. He would stride up the Kington Road of a May morning charming the air with the latest hits. His repertoire was extensive since he could whistle with remarkable accuracy any tune he'd ever heard. You could hear Ernie coming a good half mile away, a mobile flute as ever was that put the birds to shame.

14 Village Characters – the Women

The two Miss Halls spent their lives doing good. They lived in a pretty black and white house set back from the road called The Gables. It was only a step or two from ours, so we frequently saw or met them on their jaunts. They shared the house with their aged aunt Tizzie, whose word was law where her nieces were concerned. Tizzie never emerged, so I never saw her. Possibly she was an invalid. The Miss Halls were in their sixties when we first came to know them and as unlike as two sisters could be. Miss Annie, the elder, was dowdy and plain, but talked like a duchess when she condescended to converse. This wasn't often as she was always too busy attending the sick or poor, taking part in church meetings or trotting off down to the workhouse with food or presents for the inmates, on which occasions she wore long black boots. She once told us that she had completed her education in Germany, like so many upper class girls. Nowadays, with workhouses abolished and the poor better cared for, she would have had no similar place in society, though knowing her interests she would have doubtless found a niche.

Her sister Miss Maggie was different and would have been good looking in her younger days. She was sociable within the conventions and greeted all comers with a smile. Her custom on meeting was to drop a curtsy, even to small children, and to chatter away about flowers. She was quite a botanist and once escorted me down the Kington Road to show me a greater celandine. Like her sister she usually wore black, topped with a wide-brimmed hat, though Miss Annie favoured a bonnet of more sober design. They were both, you supposed, in perpetual mourning for their elders. At any rate their costume hardly varied between summer and winter. They gave the impression of surviving on a minimal income, most of which, presumably, went on the rent for the house. 'When I was a little girl,' Miss Maggie once told my sisters, 'I was made to eat so much bread and butter that I never had room for cake.'

She belonged to that cakeless and joyless brigade of Victorian children living in the shadow of elders and betters, who regarded all pleasure as sinful. But if they were the losers the village poor were the gainers and if there is such a place as heaven, as they fervently believed, their place in it was assured.

A rather different Miss Annie appeared at the annual children's fancy dress party. She would then seat herself at the piano and play the music for Sir Roger de Coverley; perhaps after all her childhood had not been so devoid of pleasure as people thought. When the WI presented a scene from *The Mill on the Floss* in

Hereford, the Miss Halls provided the ladies taking part, who included my mother, with genuine crinolines.

Miss Simmonds was a strange woman who lived by herself in a curious old house and dressed in the style of the eighteen eighties. She was then, like the Miss Halls, in her sixties and hadn't changed her way of dressing since she was a girl. She behaved like Miss Havisham in *Great Expectations*, except that she'd never been engaged – at least, if she had, nobody knew. She appeared to have no relations. Her sole companion was her sheepdog Rosie who accompanied her on walks. She rarely talked and in consequence was ignored by the villagers, including the louts, who, surprisingly, rarely made fun of her as she tottered along. Her house stood endwise on to the Kington Road and was every bit as odd in appearance as she was herself. It was surrounded by a fence which precluded entrance, while a creeper grew over the walls. She kept chickens, never went to church and my small sisters were the only guests she ever entertained. I wish I knew more about her.

Ella Leather was at the centre of social life long before we came to Weobley.

The author's mother (left) with Mabel Hope and Ellen Foster in their costumes for *The Mill on the Floss.*

She was the president of the local WI and an authority on folk-lore, about which she had written a book later to become a classic: *The Folk-lore of Herefordshire*. A lady of tireless energy, her slim tall figure could be seen daily calling on neighbours, or arranging meetings with WI officials. It was clear, even then, that she had once been good looking, though she gave little thought to her appearance. She was never happy except when doing and never seemed to relax or waste her time. She lived at Castle House, a big square edifice, behind the ruins, with her husband, the colonel, a solicitor and agent for Lloyds Bank.

Ella Leather kept a number of middle-white pigs; for ever to be seen grubbing round the roots of the oaks, which lined the approach to the ruins, opposite Jim Basset's slaughterhouse. Whether she ever sold them I do not know; some said she kept them to show. She died in 1928 having spent most of her life in Weobley.

One evening I was invited with my mother and other members of the WI to hear a talk by Lady Petrie. Egypt and Tut-ankh-amun were much in the news, so we all went along to learn more. Though the names of Howard Carter and Lord Carnarvon were by now familiar to most people, Sir Flinders Petrie was still regarded as the greatest living Egyptologist. But we were doomed to disappointment. Lady Petrie avoided mention of Tut-ankh-amun and concerned herself solely with his prehistoric forbears. It was all rather like going to hear about the king and being fobbed off with the history of his Saxon ancestors.

Anne Davies was born long before anyone else I ever knew, in the eighteen twenties. She had already passed the century mark in 1922 and clearly recalled the last election held in the town, as the village then ranked. That was when Weobley supplied Parliament with two members, ten years before the Reform Act. Then at least fifty mansions were pulled down and Weobley became a backwater like other former boroughs. On one occasion a photograph of a mantelpiece which had somehow been saved appeared in *Country Life*, but so much had been destroyed that only Anne recalled the appearance of the old town.

She was tiny and still active for all her great age, talked willingly to everyone and always wore a smile. What a pity there was nobody to take her photograph.

Mrs Johnson kept the sweet and paper shop at the top of the street, where she was assisted by her look-alike daughter. She was short and plump like Mrs Tiggy-Winkle and always wore glasses. She was eternally busy, whether collecting bundles of newspapers and penny dreadfuls from Tom Pugh or serving several customers at once, yet she never became flustered and greeted everyone by name.

Favourite sweets were gobstoppers, which Mrs Johnson considered rude and renamed golf balls, though nobody, least of all herself, had ever seen a real golf ball, much less a golf course. Packets of 'tobacco', composed of coconut, together with liquorice pipes, sold for a halfpenny and were always in demand. Nobody could afford to spend much, though young women were prepared to fork out twopence for *Peg's Paper*, which provided them at second hand with the romance they missed in life. Boys expended a like amount on *Robin Hood* and *Buffalo Bill*, while tiny tots bought *Tiger Tim's Weekly*.

Mrs Johnson never took a holiday. The furthest she walked was into the parlour at the back of the shop, which was as small as that of Ginger and Pickles, with a bronze set of scales on the counter. When my uncle Ernest called and asked for a whole pound of sweets, Mrs Johnson was hard put to hold back her tears. Never before had she received such a staggering order and she treated him like a visitor from space.

Waiting outside the shop you would find old Tommy 'Oodle' who claimed to have served in the army all over the world. 'Where d'yer shirt come from, Tommy?' the village boys would inquire with a grin. 'Hindia,' he'd mumble. 'An' yer jacket?' 'Hafrica.' Who he was I never knew.

Emmie loved Weobley where, for the first time in her life, she was encouraged to spread her wings at whist drives and dances. She once won a prize for fancy dress, when I accompanied her to Hereford to be photographed after begging a lift in Jim Basset's van. It was election day and Jim leaned out and shouted to Liberal supporters 'Vote for Shepperson!' (the Conservative candidate). But by then the Midland Bus Company had linked the village with Hereford and business began to go down. So Emmie had to leave us, and took a cook's job in Swansea. At the moment of parting she broke down in tears in front of us children, for she'd never before been away from home. Above all she was going to miss my elder sister who had always been her favourite, but I missed her too. No more picnics to Shoal's Bank, when I bought her a *Buffalo Bill* instead of *Peg's Paper* and she didn't complain. No more pointing out a kestrel hovering which, since her eyesight was so poor, she couldn't see. No more Emmie to see my point of view when others didn't. No Emmie to flatter me when I didn't deserve it.

Mention of Shoal's Bank reminds me of Meddie, because that's where she lived. Meddie – her real name was Metcalfe – came weekly to do our washing and that of our neighbours the Manleys as well. She was Eric the Cowboy's grannie. I had nicknamed Eric 'the cowboy' after discussing our futures in the light of our favourite reading which was *Buffalo Bill*. We had promptly decided that we would like to go west. 'We might meet,' Eric had added, with a faraway look in his eye. To be a cowboy chasing Indians, could anything have been more exciting than that? Except that there weren't any Indians any more

85

and cowboys weren't what they were cracked up to be. But we didn't know that and our imaginations still roamed in the never-never lands of Wyoming and Dakota.

Eric lived with his grandparents in a cottage at the top of the Bank, on the western side of the 'ill. There I met Meddie's husband, a grand old rustic, his features disguised by a white beard.

'Lived 'ere for forty nine year,' Meddie told me. 'Don't s'pose e'd care to move now.' But then retired farm labourers never moved, preferring to die in their old homes.

Meddie trudged the mile and a half to the village, disregarding the weather, arriving to turn the mangle even in the snow. She was known, my mother discovered, as Pretty Polly Metcalfe in her youth, but her face was now lined with effort, though transformed when she smiled. Meddie didn't say much. She was usually far too busy. Like so many women of her class she had learned to take life as she found it. I never heard her complain or voice an unkind sentiment about anyone.

Bachelors and spinsters were two a penny round Weobley. There were the Dents, the Pughs, the Hopes, the Taits, the Lloyds, to mention only a few. And there were also the three Griffiths sisters and their brother who lived at The Mill. That was the name of the house, but the steam mill, which still stood alongside, had closed. Despite this misfortune the family survived by selling milk and cream. Their father Al' Griffiths, who owned the orchard and used to give apples to the children as they left school, had recently died. From time to time, like latter-day Brontes, the sisters would come out and walk up the street, all except the eldest, who was deaf and preferred to live in purdah after the collapse of her affair with one of the bachelor farmers. They usually chose winter evenings when the street lights cast shadows and prevented close inspection. Then they would creep down Broad Street and engage my mother in whispered conversation, before returning like ghosts in the night. They talked together like twins and always about the same things. They never gossiped. If they couldn't think of anything nice to say about a person they would talk of something else.

'Here's master Pollard come for some cream,' their brother Johnny would announce when I called, jug in hand, at the dairy. At once, as if at a signal, one or usually both of the sisters would appear to welcome me and inquire how I did. They always seemed reluctant to accept payment and made up for it by charging sixpence for what was more than a shilling's worth.

Johnny was delicate and not up to heavy work. Every morning he visited the mill on his bicycle, presumably for the ride. When he fell ill I lent him the railway books which my father had bought in Hereford and he was

86

pathetically grateful. A little man in a cap, with a small moustache and the expression of a spaniel greeting its master: that was Johnny.

His sisters were tiny too, and the youngest still pretty. They were all in their forties when the middle one, Poppy, met a curate and married him. Unlike some sisters they always seemed to get on and never uttered a cross word. They were three angels who dedicated their lives to others and never thought or spoke a hurtful word.

Miss Wade's house had 1485, or a date near it, inscribed on the plaster above the beams. How Miss Wade had come to Weobley I never knew. She hailed from the Midlands, Staffordshire I think, and clipped her words as Midlanders do. She was the local rating officer and consequently much feared in her professional aspect.

'I'll do my best to leave you to the last,' she once promised my father when he was pressed. What was more to the point she offered to bring me some fossils. By fossils I imagined a dinosaur's bone, a mammoth's tusk or something equally impressive. Instead she produced a stone, with a minute encrustation on the corner.

The Misses Matthews lived at Pepperplock, a neat smallholding on the way to the Marsh. We often walked out to see them, accompanied by the Fosters. Their garden was gay with flowers in summer and in autumn the plum tree was heavy with fruit. There was only one snag and that was the aggressive pair of sheepdogs, in particular the one called Turk. Almost as bad was their brother Joe, who was as round as a barrel and fond of his cider.

Joe 'Mathus', as the villagers called him, was a character who mounted his horse every morning as regularly as clockwork and jogged off cowboy style to the village. It was said that he had once been a real cowboy in the USA, but such rumours could rarely be relied on. His invariable port of call was the Pugh's farmstead where he and Fred, Tom's brother, would quaff cider companionably. At times a disagreement led to high words, when those within hearing distance would pause, awed by the fury of the erstwhile cronies.

Joe was never admitted to the house when the sisters were entertaining, but was always confined to the parlour or the kitchen. He would embarrass me by coming out to see us off and breathe tipsily in my ear. 'Got any little sweet'earts? No? When I was your age I 'ad 'alf a dozen.'

So he may have, but none of the three married. The elder sister was sharp of tongue, whereas the other named 'Jinny' did what she was told. Usually she was to be seen driving a cow into the byre, while her sister dilated on the villagers' short-comings. They made butter which I collected on my bicycle. I disliked the mission because it involved braving Turk.

Queenie was easily the most attractive woman in the village. Small and neat with a winning smile and her hair tied back with a ribbon, she was an accomplished pianist and singer as well as a good tennis player. She was, I suppose, about thirty when I first knew her and she never seemed to grow older. Half the men were secretly in love with her, including myself at the ripe old age of ten. Queenie remained her mother's darling all her life and as a consequence never married despite numerous offers. Her mother once prognosticated that I would be a 'great man' one day. But she was wrong. I became a happy man instead.

15 Sportsmen and Sportswomen

Jim Bassett, the butcher, was also a sportsman who engaged in hunting and coursing and kept a pack of greyhounds. Hearing one day that he was going coursing the following Sunday, for Jim had no reservations about the Sabbath, I asked if I could go with him. I was only ten, but he agreed with a smile, provided I got up in time as he liked to start early. Sunday dawned fine and freezing, a typical misty December day, but when I arrived at the shop I found him still abed. When he eventually came down he turned back for a minute and bellowed up the stairs. 'Thora, get up! D'you 'ear me? Young Pinkie's come to court you.'

I turned red with embarrassment, for Thora was only six. When he was finally ready I went outside and joined a party of men in the pick-up. One was Fred Hope, who owned the meadow behind our garden. He too was a sportsman, who kept a racehorse and, though a grandfather, was still the best batsman around.

'Look! 'e be titherin' already!' he grinned, when he saw my teeth chattering. ''Ere, warm yerself alongside the 'ounds.' It was good advice, for the greyhounds were packed beside us in the back.

Hares were scarce round the village so Jim had made arrangements to course on a farm some miles distant. Arrived at the farm I was given a brace of dogs to hold, linked by a strap between their collars. For the first time I realised how big they were. I knew nothing about coursing so dutifully followed the others into a stubble field. Jim advanced towards the centre, holding another brace, where there was sure to be a hare. There was. Suddenly a hare got up and Jim released the greyhounds. There followed a typical course, with the hare doubling about and the hounds following close on her tail. But she was on her own territory and soon escaped through a hedge. Greyhounds hunt by sight and once their quarry was lost to view they returned somewhat shamefaced to their master.

Meantime the pair I was holding pulled me to my knees in their efforts to join the chase. We never saw another hare that morning and repaired to an outhouse for refreshment. Cider is never a warmer at the best of times and I had difficulty in swallowing the harsh amber coloured liquid which made me splutter and cough. My reaction seemed to amuse the farmer.

'Bit young, 'ent 'e, Jim?' he chuckled, refilling his glass, 'but 'e'll come to like it later, I warn.'

Coursing was a one-off. We usually went after rabbits. Rabbits were found everywhere and especially at harvest time in the corn.

'They be cuttin' up to Jim's.' someone informed me one fine August evening and the news spread like fire. Soon every man and boy was arming himself with a stick, while shopkeepers were closing early. Manley's two assistants, Tom and Harry Griffin, joined me in the street. They were a goodnatured pair and always ready for a bit of fun. Tom Griffin, who sold wild boar paste, was one of the best. Harry would sometimes pause when he found me in the storeroom and describe his experiences in the war. He had joined up with other villagers under the command of Colonel Leather and like all old soldiers loved to reminisce.

Jim Hope's wheat field was close at hand and guaranteed to hold a vast number of rabbits. By the time we all got there the field was half cut, with the binder slowly moving towards the centre. Till then not a single rabbit had broken cover, though Walter Webb, who delivered our bread and was, inevitably, nicknamed Captain, swore blind he'd seen a 'are. His claim reached the ears of Al' Annie, who earnestly entreated everyone to let the hare go. The supposed presence of a hare added to the excitement, but it was soon forgotten when the rabbits began to break. Soon everyone was chasing them as they attempted vainly to take refuge under sheaves. But the odds were against them and few escaped. As for Captain's hare, if hare it was, it must have sneaked away.

In the end no less than a hundred corpses were laid out under the big oak for Jim's inspection. Jim had brought his shotgun hopefully, but had wisely refrained from blasting off with half the village in range.

'Best take a good'un apiece,' he directed, after appraising the bag.

At his word everybody present stepped forward, stooping to grab a good'un before somebody else did.

But I didn't chase rabbits only in cornfields. During the winter I went ferreting on a friend's farm. The Powell's farm was called The Hurst and stood at the top of a steep lane some two miles distant. Mr Powell was the most genial and generous of men. His wife in spite of looking after poultry and geese, as well as a large family, was still good looking. The Powells baked their bread from their own wheat, which was sent away to be ground. The loaves were big and heavy, but tasty when generous slices were spread with butter and golden syrup. The eldest son Tom was clever and duly won a place at the High School, while his younger brother Dick came as a fee-payer. Their pretty little sister Mona lingered in the background, shy in the presence of company. The Powells, like other farming families, were in a sense cut off from the world, but we loved the farm with all the fun of climbing in the ricks or fishing for eels in the goose pond. I was sorry for Mrs Powell who never had a holiday. The best she could manage, she once told my mother, was sitting out on a chair in the sun and imagining she was by the seaside.

Rabbiting of any kind was generally regarded as a plebeian sport and both ferreting and 'cutting', as chasing rabbits in the corn was termed, were minor recreations in comparison with foxhunting.

'Oundsbecome!' I tried to digest this piece of incomprehensible information, wondering what on earth my informant was on about. It wasn't until I observed George Manley in hot pursuit of a hound which had raided his shop and was running off with a piece of bacon that intelligence dawned. Soon loud and unfamiliar accents attracted my attention.

'Where's Leathah'? The impatient query of the master of the Radnorshire and West Hereford hounds revealed that the gentry had come to town. Everywhere were horses and riders, bawling greetings in county accents and ignoring the villagers who had come out to watch. Many were women, some riding sidesaddle, with white masks for faces. They did their best to hide their fear by backing their mares and every time a child came too close shouting a shrill warning. The meet was held at Castle House, where, after entertaining the field, the colonel had arrived late, much to the master's irritation.

When the field moved off, Leonard, Tom and I followed eagerly on foot. Beyond Newton Court, hounds were put into covert. The followers meantime coffee-housed in two rings, the one consisting of farmers, the other of the gentry. The farmers wore cloth caps, tweed jackets and butcher boots, while most of the others, with the exception of the girls and women, wore pink coats and silk hats. Jim Bassett took up station with the farmers, beaming roguishly around.

Suddenly hounds gave tongue. Unseen, the fox had broken cover and next moment the field was thundering away. One young man in a bowler shouted 'Tally-ho!' as he cleared a hedge.

A disturbance ahead attracted our attention. A farmer was standing on a low wall and cursing the hunt and its members as they passed. It appeared that a newly sown field had been trampled on. It was then that I realised that hunting wasn't universally popular and feeling somewhat abashed we turned for home. Little did I think that years later Len and I would hunt too, not, at least in my case, for the pleasure of killing foxes, but purely to test my nerve. Some weeks later there was great excitement when a fox was chased into Manley's orchard. My father hurried out to photograph the scene, for nobody in those days considered the fox.

Weobley Sports was a major event in the village calendar, held on Whit Monday. The sports were held in a meadow fronting Garnstone Castle and included track and cycling events as well as horse racing. Fred Hope's entry in the latter differed from the rest in as much as it raced every time under a new name and even, on occasion, a new colour. Sometimes it was bay, at others grey and once dark chestnut. Since it invariably won nobody objected, but then all the village punters backed Fred. On my first visit to the sports at the age of eight I was knocked over by the leading horse, which fell when the crowd hemmed it in. By some fluke I wasn't injured and got up to be greeted by a grinning Thomas.

Leaving the sports in the late afternoon I joined Nana pushing my sisters in the pram. At that moment a drunk, Groucho Marx's double, leaped out from some trees, barring our way. He had apparently been taunted by a group of big-uns, who stood guffawing in the background. When the man realised that the person he had taken for one of his tormentors was in fact a lady, he described a bow and almost toppled over. Unnerved by the spectacle I ran for my life, never having encountered a drunk before.

Cricket was played on a field owned by Jim Hope and known by the curious name of the Gobbutts. Though then in his fifties, Jim, who was immensely strong, could still hit sixes. Though everyone played football the village lacked cricketers and anyone with the least pretensions as batsman or bowler was included in the team. My father used to open the innings in company with the Methodist minister, named Nicholas. The latter certainly looked the part, being tall and hairy, yet never made a score. This unfortunate circumstance didn't prevent him from scolding his son Bill, a natural batsman.

'Na, na lad!' he would chide, adopting a stance which could have done credit to W.G. Grace.

'If tha plays like yon tha'll be out. But if tha plays like this, then so be it.'

Nobody knew that the Miss Halls had a brother until Felix turned up. The sobriquet Felix was given him by the doctor, after the famous cat, from the way he hurried along. Felix was a slight figure with a straggly beard, and whenever he met someone he knew his face would light up with a smile. He even tried his hand at cricket and would make a valiant stand in the nets against the minister's slows.

'Am I bowling too fast for thee?' the latter would inquire solicitously, to which Felix, bending low over his bat, would answer 'Not yet! Not yet!'

Skilled batsmen are rare in village cricket and Fred Hope was relied upon to make the runs. Curly Davies' job was to skittle the opposition out, in which he was remarkably successful. He was a star footballer, and had he been reared in Manchester or Nottingham might well have become a professional in both games. He was christened Harry but was known confusingly both as Curly and Peter.

Though I enjoyed games, my main interest was always in sport. I roamed about the fields with an airgun, purely for pleasure, for I was far too soft-hearted to kill anything. Later, Mr Powell gave me his father's muzzle loader, for which I obtained a supply of black powder and caps. The supplier was old Mr Williams, from whom I had bought fishing tackle while we lived in Hereford, but he warned me the powder could 'burn you bad'.

Not to be outdone by the men who in winter had their football, the younger women formed a hockey club. As in cricket it was difficult to raise a team, but such was the dedication of the original members that they usually fielded a full side. Another difficulty was fixtures or mainly the lack of them. Despite challenging schools and teams of higher calibre they enjoyed considerable success. My mother, though in her forties, also turned out, though she hadn't played for years. It was a personal triumph to play against the old girls of her school and win, watched by her three sisters.

One member of the team was named Ethel, daughter of Anderson the grocer. Ethel was a doer who ran everything from dances and whist drives to village fêtes. On one occasion she elicited my services to make posters to advertise an 'Olde World Fayre'. This earned me half a crown. But thought of Ethel reminds me of her elder brother County, a flamboyant character like Bummer whom it was impossible to ignore.

County must have been in his late twenties and always wore leggings and breeches. He hunted, I believe, like Jim Bassett, which might in part have accounted for his nickname. He was the first to dub me Pinkie, when I caught my inaugural rabbit, as he was cutting his field. That he had a presence there was no denying and he behaved in some ways like a member of the gentry. I was rather afraid of him until he married, when he quietly forsook the village scene. His younger brother was known as Little County, such was the persistence of the nickname.

Weobley women's hockey team.

16 The Scholarship

The years between five and ten are perhaps the best in a boy's life, because it is then that he finds out what life is about and his place in it. He is too young to accept much responsibility, though he has come to appreciate the difference between right and wrong. He is also delightfully free, with the world as his oyster. At least that was my experience, though others were not so lucky, but when I was eleven there came a change, for now it was important to look to the future and the future meant education.

How my father came to know about scholarships I do not know, since nobody had ever won one at Weobley. The reason was that Dean was opposed to them on the curious grounds that they would rob the school of his best pupils. Undeterred by this my father bearded Dean in his den, but the latter refused to give in without a fight.

'Just see what that man wants,' he had snapped to a pupil teacher when my father called at the school. But when my father returned, supported by Philip Foster, he tried a new tack by stating that I stood no chance. As it happened I had come top of the weekly class list, but Dean removed it from the notice board and persisted with his argument. Had winning a scholarship depended on general knowledge then he conceded that my chances would have been improved. As it was, it would be best to forget the whole matter. My father declined to listen to Dean and sent me to Miss Manley for coaching. Later, coaching was frowned upon as giving unfair advantage. My father's efforts on my behalf had repercussions throughout the county when the education authorities were informed about Dean's intransigence. Rawle, the headmaster of Norton Canon, came into the shop in high dudgeon, only to sober down when he was acquainted with the facts. So I was duly entered and joined the other candidates one May in Hereford at Scudamore, the leading primary school.

Everyone was very nervous and in attempting to settle down I was considerably disconcerted by the behaviour of the invigilator, a big man with a florid face which contrasted oddly with his mop of white hair. He crept round on tiptoe, like a fox on the prowl, pausing every so often to look over someone's shoulder. I found it quite unnerving.

Sitting an examination is a demoralising experience as I know after years of martyrdom. Little did I realise that the scholarship was merely the bottom rung of a ladder which I should be required to climb for years. Good examinees are by nature calm people, who are oblivious of the rustle of paper, the interrup-

94

tion of candidates going to the toilet or the sound of the clock ticking away. The ancient Chinese, we are told, sat public examinations, while incarcerated in huts for long periods. Food was passed under the door, so at least they were not called on to endure the intrusion of invigilators. When the results were announced successful candidates were rewarded with official posts, much as in Britain in the days of civil service examinations.

Of the papers set in the scholarship examination I recall very little, except that they were coloured pink and that in English we were required to answer questions on a passage from Ivanhoe. I do remember fairly letting myself go on a question inquiring what books we had read recently. By some lucky chance I had come across The Adventures of Ulysses, which had made a big impression. Doubtless the fact that I could spell the long Greek names weighed with the examiners. At any rate, on June 10 1925, my mother's birthday, I was informed that I was required to attend at the High School for an oral examination, which meant that I had passed.

When the villagers heard they were nonplussed, as none of their number had won a scholarship before. Some were jealous, realising too late what their children had missed. Most were indifferent, content with their lives. Ambition was lacking in most of my contemporaries, since there appeared to be no means of bettering themselves. Further jealousy was aroused by the way I was treated, as a kind of local hero, by the Verdins at the Garnstone fête, and Dean, the hypocrite, called me out before the school for fulsome praise.

In 1924 the British Empire Exhibition was held at Wembley and Dean arranged for a school party to attend. His warning that we would need 'at least ten shillings pocket money' had struck me at the time as an awful lot. Instead we went on a family holiday to Mumbles, while Emmie returned for a fortnight from Swansea to renew acquaintance with old friends and to look after the shop. The following year, as a reward for winning the scholarship, my father decided to take my brother and me to see the exhibition which had been extended for a further year.

Rooms were booked with a lady we knew, who had lived in Hereford, but whose husband, a teacher, had recently died. She had advertised rooms in the Hereford Times, which also attracted the Bants. The husband, a large man with a puce face, was an ex-member of the metropolitan police force. He suffered from his heart so was advised to take things quietly. His wife was more lively and spoke with a pronounced cockney accent. The pair had retired near Weobley, though we hadn't met them before. Whenever we got lost in London and wished to ask the way Bant would gravely approach any available officer and salute like a soldier before speaking. This, we were told, intimated to the other that Bant too had served in the force.

Our landlady lived in a nice house in Streatham with her younger daughter, a girl in her late teens. She was an attractive woman with her hair dyed black and did her best to make us comfortable. She had two daughters. The elder, who was plainer and married, was a snob and professed to recall nothing of her life in Hereford.

'But I don't remembah!' she said in Bloomsbury accents, to her mother's embarrassment. 'No, I don't remembah at all.'

The younger was a shy girl and whenever you asked her about London she would reply 'I hate Trafalgar Square. I simply hate it.'

For lunch we went to a Lyons café opposite Big Ben. The Bants came with us and also joined us for tea, usually in the vicinity of St James's Park. Tommy and I rather liked the park, since it was green like Hope's meadow. We had rapidly become disillusioned with the general drabness of the capital city and the novelty of catching tubes and trams soon began to wear off. Seeing the sights wasn't much more alluring, and we gazed dull-eyed at the paintings in the Tate and National Galleries and enjoyed only the zoo. Westminster Abbey I found depressing with its graves and tombs.

We were impressed by the Horse Guards, if not with Buckingham Palace, but most by the pipers at the Torchlight Tattoo. The latter took place in the evening at Wembley, after we'd visited the exhibition. Extending it for a second year had proved a flop, so there were very few crowds to worry us. Listless Africans and Asians manned the stalls, whose allurements I have long since forgotten. More to our taste was the amusement park, where our eyes were caught by the scenic railway and giant racer. We persuaded our father to take us on the latter, though none of us had ever experienced the thrills of a big dipper. To begin with we were lulled into a sense of pleasurable anticipation when the cars rose slowly towards the sky. Suddenly the sky ended and we dropped like a stone.

'Hold your breath and hang on!' my father shouted, as the cars began to climb again. Three times we challenged gravity and after rattling through a tunnel came to a halt.

The one thing I did enjoy at the exhibition was being privileged to mount the cab of the Great Western Railway's Caerphilly Castle, at that time Britain's most prestigious locomotive.

One evening we went to a cinema, which featured a dark villainous vamp called Evelyn. During the course of the film she not only made love to several men, but also committed murder. 'Type of woman I don't like,' my father had commented as we retired to bed.

When, after a fortnight, our first London visit ended Tom and I were frankly relieved. It was gratifying on reaching home to be able to boast about our adventures to our schoolmates, some of whom had never even seen a river,

Boys Secondary School, Hereford.

Hereford. Photo Series.

The Boy's High School, Hereford.

much less the sea or a town, but the experience had merely given me a distaste for urban life which has never left me.

But my thoughts were already turning elsewhere, to the new school I was due to enter in September. Leonard was coming with me too as a fee-payer.

'I expect those are the studies,' I had confided to Leonard, when we gazed through the railings at the red-brick edifice, built on waste ground near the Cattle Market, some weeks before the autumn term commenced. My knowledge of schools above the primary level was based on Tom Brown's Schooldays, which I had won as a prize at the children's fancy dress. Alas there was little resemblance between the High School and Rugby and I was in for a painful shock.

17 Train Boys

In order to get to the High School there was no alternative but to cycle each morning to Moorhampton station. It was only three and a half miles but not all on the flat. In places the gradient was so steep that you couldn't manage it and had to get off and walk.

Len and I usually left my home before 7.30. The train left promptly at 8.10 and there wasn't another for hours. During spring and summer the ride could be pleasant and we found much to interest us. Peewits nested among the furrows and a pair of owls in a blasted oak. There was also a peartree growing beside the road at the top of the final drop, whose sharp fruit quenched our thirst on hot days. In autumn, the champion ploughman would acknowledge us with a cheery tilt of the chin as we passed.

When the weather was bad, or so frosty that we were obliged to wear scarves to protect our ears, Len's father would sometimes transport us in his motorbike and sidecar. If he let us down, as he occasionally did, when he was obliged to attend to other duties, Len would arrive late and we would breast the rise by Shoal's Bank to hear the train rattling down the valley. Then we had to put on an extra spurt and abandon our bicycles outside the station, instead of leaving them in the garage of a house nearby.

Moorhampton was a typical country station. Like others of its kind it had a pretty garden, tended by the porter, as well as the stationmaster if not otherwise engaged. When on duty the stationmaster wore a smart black uniform and busman style cap with a peak of gold braid. In the twenties, stationmasters were men of importance and those in the top rank at famous London termini sported silk hats when royalty was about.

The stationmaster had two daughters. The younger was a bright little thing of six or seven, ready to kiss the boys when they held up a sprig of mistletoe above the station entrance and levied an embrace as the price of access. Not so the shy elder sister who was a beauty of fifteen. She always wore a red tam over her blonde hair and drew admiring glances whenever she boarded the train.

At the station, in addition to the master's daughters, would be gathered a dozen boys and girls, ranging in age from eleven to eighteen. They had walked from their homes in the local villages and were mostly farmers' sons and daughters, with a sprinkling of the children of men employed as gardeners or chauffeurs at the big houses. Apart from the stationmaster's daughters they were all bound for the boys' and girls' high schools in Hereford and wore the distinguishing red and blue ringed caps or bonnets. I was long enamoured, at a respectful distance, of a girl with a Mona Lisa smile.

One handsome youth sporting the gold and blue cap of the Cathedral School was an army officer's son and was dressed in a dark suit and longs. Most of the High School boys still wore shorts, from which their knees projected like haunches of uncooked meat. The officer's son liked to show off by performing feats of daring. On one occasion he dropped a large stick on the line just as the train was approaching. When the porter warned him of possible damages he hopped down on to the rails as swift as a bird and quickly retrieving the stick hopped safely back again.

'Come on! There's Florrie!' a plump youth shouted as the train drew in. As the guard blew the whistle a laughing throng of adolescents crammed into the compartment where the girls were sitting to a chorus of giggles and squeals. Len and I joined the group of boys staring out of the windows of an adjoining carriage.

'What's your name, son?' a big freckled-faced lout demanded. When I told him he grinned. 'Daft name that, son. Sounds like a parrot. Where d'you come from?' 'Weobley,' I answered. 'Bright place that,' he grunted contemptuously. 'What be there to do there?' 'Sweep the tide out,' a fat boy answered, carefully removing and polishing his glasses. It was the first time I had heard mention of Weobley Docks, but it certainly wasn't the last.

'Can you fight, son?' The good-looking boy with high cheekbones regarded me narrowly out of black slit eyes.

''ere, give us that bloody stick,' a thin youth seated in the corner twittered, tugging out the baton from the blind. Meantime his companion, a powerfully built lad with a shock of fair hair, dutifully extracted another from the blind by his head and handed it over.

'Now us can 'ave a band,' the other grinned cadaverously through a row of broken teeth.

'Oh I wonder where my baby is tonight,' he warbled in a nasal falsetto, 'Oh I wonder how my darling looks in tights.' For a minute he drummed a tattoo on the window pane before throwing the two sticks out on to the track.

'Blinds bent no good without sticks,' he added, tearing down the fabric and tossing it out too.

'Fun an' games goin' on next door,' he leered over his shoulder.

''ere, let's 'ave a dekko,' the fat boy interrupted, pushing out his head.

'Eh-up 'e wants the tickets,' the freckled boy warned, as the collector opened the door at Credenhill.

''fraid I fergot mine,' the short boy grinned. 'I'll be sure to bring it tomorrow.'

'Ent never 'ad one.' The thin youth's eyes were the picture of innocence. 'Somebody stole it last term.'

But before the young official could protest the train began to move.

'Can you fight, son?' Slit-eyes reiterated, banging me hard across the chest. ''ereford! 'ereford! All change! All change!'

In addition to fights and bullying in the carriages there was sometimes worse to face. A pair of worthies, one with a superior accent who attended the Cathedral School, the other a farmer's hulking son, had a habit of following little boys into an empty compartment and as soon as the train was clear of the station began to threaten them. When they attacked me I put up my fists and threatened to pull the communication cord. Such unexpected resistance had a salutary effect and from then on I was left alone.

The High School was a good mile from Hereford station so you had to hurry to get there in time. There was actually a direct way, but it crossed private land, so you took the route through the abandoned churchyard, opposite the Hop Pole inn. Passing the Girls' High School, two little damsels who remembered me from Miss Kear's got off their bikes and gave me a friendly wave.

Being a train-boy had other disadvantages in addition to being bullied. To begin with we were precluded from taking part in games, since to do so meant either missing the train or travelling back to Hereford on Saturdays. The same applied to the Cadet Corps (though few were keen on that) as well as school concerts or plays. We were not alone in this. Many children travelled by train in those days from all over the county, while the rest often cycled long distances. Travelling in from Moorhampton was bad enough, but some had to come from Hay. Whether any travelled farther I do not remember, but to get to Hay station by seven of a winter morning cannot have been pleasant for those who did. One who did was a boy called Eckley whose father kept a stud. Eckley was always neatly dressed and impressed me immensely when he told me the farm covered more than a thousand acres. I longed to view this hillfarm and Len and I made tentative arrangements to cycle over. Alas, we never went and when I met Eckley many years later at a horse show he invited me again to visit him and his family, but he died before I could go.

Setting out on a winter's morning with only the glimmer of our carbide lights to dispel the gloom and returning late again in the dark was bad enough without being faced by a mountain of homework after a hurried meal. There were normally three subjects on each of which you were supposed to spend not more than forty minutes. Usually it was more, so you got to bed late, only to be roused early ready to begin the dreary treadmill again. It was hard on my mother, who not only had to rise at an even more ungodly hour but to pack sandwiches as well.

Every afternoon at a quarter to four a boy would put up his hand and inquire whether it was time for train boys. More often than not a master would deny that it was, in the mistaken belief that most train boys were malingerers. As a result we were often obliged to run the whole way to the station. Once I fell and gashed my knee, which didn't recover for ages.

There were advantages too in being a train boy. It was nice to leave the school behind, particularly at the weekends, when it was possible to return to country life and share adventures with former cronies. Leonard and I were privileged to hunt rabbits with Jim the terrier and enjoy opportunities to go fishing. Len's father no longer restricted his expeditions to Sarnesfield pool and Letton, but now roamed further afield to Monnington on Wye. The possession of a motorcycle combination broadened his horizon, while I cycled down the Brook to Stretford to use a fly to fish for trout.

The train was a good place to do homework, provided you were left in peace. Older boys would help you, if they weren't too busy with their own tasks. It was a curious fact that the lower a boy stood in the social order the better seemed to be his brains. Until scholarships were offered to enable boys from poor homes to obtain a secondary education, much potential talent lay fallow. One boy called Stokes who travelled with me in the train came top in the award of cadetships to Cranwell. He followed in the wake of the Cleland brothers, one of whom became a group captain. He was a brilliant scientist and a willing help in trouble to people like me. It is sad to think how lack of social graces hinders progress or stifles talent even today.

Leonard and I were victims of the General Strike in 1926. Fortunately it took place in summer and even more fortunately it didn't last long. There was great excitement when reports were broadcast of duchesses collecting tickets in trams or buses, while ordinary citizens volunteered to drive trains. It is extraordinary how a crisis brings out the best in people, as happened in World Wars I and II. Baldwin, the prime minister, was the man of the hour and everyone looked to him to save the country. Meantime we pedalled the twelve and a half miles to Hereford and back, though we were sometimes late when held up by cattle. The new headmaster forgave us, as anyone would in the circumstances.

Farmers filled the train on Wednesdays, when we were frequently the butt of their coarse good humour. One elderly man would burst into song after imbibing heavily in celebration of a successful deal. I still remember the punch line, though I have long since forgotten the rest. It was rendered with tearful feeling: 'When the fields are white with daisies I'll come home.'

Another farmer would slap a boy's thighs and glare round belligerently. 'What, I asks, 'as England to fear with boys like these.' He would exclaim. He would next proceed to forecast that if war came again it would be against the French, not the Germans as previously.

Yet another would announce that he was divided as to whether to send his son to the High or the Cathedral School, mentioning in his favour that ''e's a devil to fight you.'

We boosted the High School. But he said someone else had preferred the other. The Cathedral School charged eleven pounds a term, as against the High School's four. It also ranked as a public school. But whether the farmer knew anything of this was exceedingly doubtful.

One farmer, dressed in velveteen, I heartily disliked. He would give a boy a sixpence to buy a packet of Players to hand round to his school-mates. If girls chanced to be present he would embarrass me with coarse remarks or obscene references to my short trousers. He wore a flat cap and had a brown moustache, and my heart sank when he appeared, but on the whole I liked the farmers, and Velveteen was very much the exception.

18 Hereford High School Boys and Masters

The scholarship boys were ranged in order and it was only when I was told by the form master to occupy the first desk that I realised that I had come out top. This soon proved a doubtful distinction since whenever I failed to answer a question correctly it made me the butt of the master's wit. He could always on such occasions raise a titter by opining that the examiners had been looking at the list upside down.

The form master, Daniels, was a big man, inclining to fat and, like most of his colleagues, had served in the war. The war had been over for seven years, though in Daniels' case you would never have guessed it. He treated the form with heavy humour, like a squad of recruits, or, by way of variety, like convicts, but nobody minded and his methods worked, so that he was missed when he left to be a headmaster at a school in the West Indies.

The scholarship boys included the Edwards brothers, who cycled in daily from Hampton Bishop; Burland, a bumptious Yorkshire lad, who was good at everything including games and music, being a polished performer on the violin; and Smith. Smith's father was an engine driver who, while I was waiting for the train at the station, climbed down from the cab of an impressive express engine and introduced himself. Then there was Fatty Jones, who impressed us all by weighing eight stone six. Only Booth was heavier at nine stone two, but he was one of the fee-payers. Booth subsequently attained the rank of chief constable, while another boy Carver, who also intended to join the force, was known by the masters as 'Policeman'. He, like Booth, was aged fifteen and noted for his skill at soccer. So was the farmer's son handsome Reg Barrett, who tipped the scales at seven and a half stone, which made the form master inquire jokingly whether his mother fed him on porridge. The rest of us weighed between five and six stone, while one boy weighed even less than that.

Wheatley, whose father kept the impressive looking Hop Pole Inn in Commercial Road, was also fifteen and could squeeze tears whenever he was asked a question. He had the reputation of being a skilled boxer so was treated as cock of the form. His superior accent helped.

Masters arriving every forty minutes were, for most of us, something new. I had only known Dean and a couple of mistresses, but now there was a master for every subject. At the time masters were required to visit each form room in turn, though later the roles of master and pupil were reversed and the latter went to the appropriate subject room.

The schoolmasters at the High School were exceptional characters, the liveliest of all being the English master William Witts who, on my first day, made a dramatic entry.

'My name's Witts and don't you forget it.' The dark man with the long upper lip regarded us reflectively. 'I've come to teach you English grammar. We will begin with the verb. The verb is a doing word. Look – I walk.' Suiting action to the word he began rapidly perambulating up and down the room.

'You see I'm still walking. I haven't stopped yet. This is the present tense. Now you see I've stopped.' The thirty pairs of eyes immediately came to rest.

'Of course,' the voice went on, 'all verbs aren't action words. I mean err is a

The High School staff in 1933.
Back row: E.R. Wood, K.J. Jones
Middle row: A.F. Watson, E.G. Wilson, W. Witts, D. Borar, J.I. Stephens
Front row: W.E. Birde-Jones, A.J. Heale, R.G. Ruscoe (headmaster), J.W. Ashton (senior master), A.M. Hartley

verb and I could say, if I wanted, instead of 'I walk', 'I err.' In other words I William Witts MA Oxford sometimes make mistakes. Oh, but you say, impossible! No, not impossible. To err is human.'

When we got into Five B Witts became our form master and was responsible, in addition to English, for our religious knowledge. 'Jesus Christ, and I say it quite reverently, was the greatest sportsman who ever lived,' he once claimed in connection with the turning of water into wine.

On another occasion when the phrase 'possessed of the devil' turned up he illustrated its meaning from an incident in his family. 'My little boy is fond of chocolate blancmange and yesterday during dinner he flew into a rage, when he found it was all gone. He was of course possessed of a devil. So I took down his trousers and cast the devil out.' The form dissolved in merriment, but the lesson was driven home.

The cleverest boy in the school was Offler, at least on the arts side. He won a scholarship to Cambridge at the age of fifteen and was rather feared by the masters. One morning Witts burst into the form room in a state of mock anger.

'I'd give three of my fingers – no, three of my toes,' he corrected quickly, 'just to prove Offler wrong.'

And nobody ever did, as Welbourne the head of his Cambridge college acknowledged when I told him the story after the war, in which Offler had further distinguished himself .

Offler had a head of hair like a Greek god, consisting of tight blond curls above a broad forehead. When roused he would roar like an angry archbishop, as happened when a boy called Davies tripped him up during a game of playground football. His thunderous rebuke: 'If you can't play fair don't play at all!' is still ringing in my ears.

Witts told us he was thirty-seven, but he sometimes behaved like a teenager. He once came singing and dancing into the room, warbling the pop song of the moment: 'VALENCIA!' During the appalling winter of 1928–1929 when the water pipes froze and the temperature in the form rooms went down to minus he would jump to his feet and take the class in a session of violent PT. He was a religious fundamentalist, as well as a Mason, and once cycled to Weobley to preach in a chapel.

Whereas Witts was good humoured and never got into a temper Heale the history master frequently did. He was short and clean shaven with a face like a Roman and a gravelly turn of speech. He insisted on absolute obedience in class and was liable to blow his top at the first sign of indiscipline. Even when he was disposed to be genial it was wisest not to presume. Like Daniels he indulged in heavy humour and his butts were often the same boys. For some reason the very mention of Pontrilas, a station on the Welsh border, was guaranteed to raise a laugh. Unfortunately for the boys who caught the train there it arrived at Hereford at 9.15. This meant, of course, that they were always late for school and Heale never let them forget it.

'Where do you come from, my beauty?' he'd inquire innocently of the first latecomer as he joined the class.

'Pontrilas – eh? And that's why you're late?'

'The train doesn't get in till a quarter past nine,' the boy would explain for the hundredth time knowing full well what was coming. As he started to go to his place Heale would call him back with a broad grin. 'Just a minute, my beauty, haven't you forgotten something?' With a look of resignation the boy would then begin to intone the lines from *As you like it*.

And then the whining schoolboy with satchel
And shining morning face creeping like snail
Unwillingly to school.

'Creeping like snail,' the history master would chuckle, savouring the word.

Another butt of Heale's humour was a boy named Wright who he claimed was always wrong. He usually was and became a kind of celebrity in a minor way.

It was dangerous to yawn in Heale's presence, no matter how tired you felt. 'Did I see a boy gape?' he'd demand in affected astonishment. 'Perhaps two periods of detention will help to wake you up.' Yet for all his badinage Heale was a good teacher and obtained outstanding exam results.

The tactics of Pym Wilson, the geography and art master, were equally effective but very different.

'Eh out, 'e's starin'!' a boy would whisper paling before the master's steady gaze. Pym was of medium height, poker-backed and moved rather slowly. Unlike most of the other masters he wasn't a graduate and shared with Birdie Jones, who taught sums to Lower Two, and little Watson, the woodwork master, the doubtful privilege of remaining ungowned. Though he lacked drive and efficiency his lessons were often memorable for a different reason. When a boy was not attending he would pause in what he was saying and stare him out of countenance. The ruse was invariably successful. Most boys can cope with anger and sarcasm, but Pym's pitiless, unwavering stare was calculated to disconcert even the most hardened sinners. On occasion the stare would persist for five minutes before the lesson resumed. Pym rarely rebuked a boy, except for untidiness, when he would comment icily 'This piece of work displays a lack of moral fibre. I will not take it.'

As the school lacked a qualified PT instructor, physical training was taken by Whitehead, a dapper ex-captain who had won an MC and talked with a military drawl. None of us enjoyed the senseless bending and stretching, and commands to 'Watch that Charlie!' A 'charlie' we soon learnt was an Army expression for round shoulders and the gallant officer banged me so hard on the back that I frequently toppled over.

Whitehead was an extrovert, healthy and good looking, and when he joined in a game of football he outclassed the best players. 'Dirty little devil!' he'd grin when some lout tried to trip him, always patently conscious of his own superior skill. Indeed there seemed to be no end to Whitehead's remarkable talents for he was also by far the best pianist in the school, yet our progress in Latin was so abysmally funereal that I sometimes suspected that he wasn't the best scholar in the world.

Despite his popularity and surface frankness, like all other masters, he fought shy of sex. 'What does "lie with me" mean sir?' a boy would inquire innocently when we were reading in the Bible about Joseph and Potiphar's wife. On such occasions Whitehead's embarrassment was so painful that it communicated itself to the form. 'It means – it sort of means – how can I put it? Er – sin with me,' he would end lamely. It was the same with 'who pisseth

The High School prefects in 1928.
Back row: G.K. Cade, A.A. Haimes, E.G. Beavan, H.S. Offler
Front row: D.S. Davies, I.M.R. Owen

against the wall'. 'Oh dear, here's our old rude phrase again!' he would comment, blushing faintly.

Hill was Whitehead's successor, a mild little man with an exiguous moustache precisely like the dude advertising Sharp's Creamy Toffee. So he was nicknamed 'Monty' from the start, mainly in respect of the way he talked because unlike the other masters he was clearly the product of a public school. He certainly knew a lot of Latin, far more than Whitehead, but then he had drunk from the fountain head at Oxford. We were reading the second book of the *Aeneid* at the time and he did his level best to get it across, but it was a forlorn hope since we lacked the requisite grammatical foundation. His attempts to take PT were a riot, as he had no sense of discipline, but he was popular just because he was so kind and gentlemanly in comparison with his colleagues.

When Witts observed us through the window of Five B forming a scrum and ignoring Hill's whistle and cries of 'Gross Foul,' he made it his business to reprimand us when we came in. 'D'you think it's quite fair to rag a new master like that?' he demanded severely. 'You wouldn't try it on with me, now would you?' Everyone agreed and life became less hectic for Monty. When I left he inscribed a passage from Cicero and another from Horace in my album. Once, he inadvertently left a letter from a lady friend open on his desk and everyone went up to read it. Suddenly he realised what they were doing. His cheeks turned scarlet and he swiftly pocketed the *billet-doux*.

'Ashton's fair!' a farmer's son once observed and it was true that the master who taught mathematics dealt fairly, on the whole, with his hard-working charges. In a former age boys had suffered from the tyranny of the Classics. Now it was the turn of so-called 'elementary mathematics.' I never understood why mathematics was so described, whereas other subjects, though taught at an elementary level, were not. Classics had been dropped on non-utilitarian grounds in all but the public schools. Yet geometry, algebra (which Ashton pronounced 'elgebra'), arithmetic and trigonometry were, for the most part, equally useless to most of us, yet we were drilled in quadratic equations, progressions and such as if our careers depended on it. Jack Ashton was tall and wore *pince nez,* somewhat like the *Magnet* form master Mr Quelch. He was also a major in the cadet corps, in which Whitehead had also served. His flights of irony were couched in a north Midland accent and rarely missed the mark. To speak, if it was only to borrow a ruler, was immediately punished as a heinous sin. As a result it was difficult not to gain something from Ashton's rigorous efficiency.

In addition to teaching mathematics throughout the school Ashton was the unofficial school detective. Should a boy be involved in trouble Ashton was sure to sort it out, pulverising the victim with queries that would not have disgraced a barrister. His standing joke when we were doing stocks and shares was to remark 'You never know: one day you may have a few thousands lying idle.'

If Ashton was efficient, Dai Borar the science master was brilliant. Like so many gifted people he was unable to communicate his knowledge to his pupils so only the clever, like Stokes, benefitted from his teaching. Perhaps we didn't try hard enough, but physics demanded a competence in mathematics which few possessed. Borar was a tall man, thin, with a leonine head. He was always affable and spoke with a soft South Walian accent. Something of an athlete he would, on rare occasions, join the bowlers at the nets. When on duty during lunchtime he would never turn a boy away who came up to seek his aid with a mathematical problem. As a consequence everyone liked Dai.

Wattie Watson, who taught woodwork, was easily the most popular master in the school. In physique he was insignificant and never lost his temper except with boys who damaged his tools. In Wattie's eyes tools were things of beauty, fit only for craftsmen and worthy of being treated with respect.

'I will give you four periods of detention' he would rap, his brown toothbrush moustache bristling. 'Just look at the grooves you've made in this plane!'

But such were rare occasions. Even when louts, bored with carpentry, picked up laths and began to fence he'd merely reprove them like a mother chiding a bunch of fractious children. 'Now, now, me lads!' he'd censure gently 'Now me-lads, me-lads!'

Wattie was never happier than when talking about ships and the sea, his ancestral heritage. His father had been a sea captain and he told me his last words were 'Look at that ship there, in the sunset,' so when I made a model sailing boat he shared my enthusiasm.

If he caught you miscutting a piece of wood he would glance over your shoulder and gently chide. 'Oh me-lad, but ah wouldn't!' And, of course, he was always right.

The French master, Hartley, came from the north. He didn't so much teach us French as frighten French into us. He was tall and brisk with a clipped military moustache, which somehow consorted ill with his broad Lancastrian accent. When he pronounced the 'butch' of butcher to rhyme with 'touch' it soon got around and Witts fairly brought the house down when we were reading *Julius Caesar* by loudly declaiming that word in a speech of Mark Antony's, as Hartley would have pronounced it.

Schools are proud of their athletes and sportsmen. Reg Perks of Worcester-shire and England fame was, for a time, in the same form as I was. That was in 1926 when we were both in IV B. As the school lacked a ground of its own, cricket was played at the racecourse. During the General Strike, when I cycled

The High School 1st XI, 1926–7.
Back row: I.W. Grafton, A.G. Cleland, W.L. Owen, C.J. Brecknell, W.J. Tudor, J.L. Hodgkiss.
Front row: H.R. Worgen, J. Birch, V.H. Jones (captain), E.F. Stubbs, R.J. Perks.

to school, Reg would borrow my bicycle and ride down to the racecourse with me sitting on the bar. He was far too good to play with junior boys and usually turned out with the fifth and sixth forms.

Reg's father was the groundsman at the racecourse, a curmudgeonly old fellow who was said to keep his son practising at the nets till kingdom come. The High School masters were much in awe of him and with good reason. Few of them were cricketers and most scarcely knew the ball from the bat. During one match in which I was playing, with Pym in charge, a boy held his bat in such a ludicrous fashion that Perks senior, who was watching, abandoned his roller, strolled over to the wicket, and ignoring Pym, calmly demonstrated the correct procedure for making a stroke.

Discipline at the High School was weak under Crompton, a small grey-moustached mathematician whose duties seemed to begin and end with dismissing the assembly after prayers. Apart from that we were practically unaware of his existence, though doubtless a gifted boy like Bailey benefitted from his teaching. Bailey was Offler's mathematical counterpart and after taking high honours became an actuary, whereas Offler became a professor. But during Crompton's regime the number of detentions mounted daily until there was scarcely time for miscreants to work them off, but when Crompton retired the new headmaster Ruscoe promptly dealt with the situation. Like Keate at Eton he resorted to beating every boy who had more than ten. The result was a remarkable drop in the number of detentions and a notable improvement in the morale of the school. Not content with viewing things from the top, Ruscoe insisted on teaching too. He, like Crompton, was a Cambridge mathematician and his appointment marked a new stage in the history of the school. In the end Ruscoe became the instigator of many remarkable achievements, all of which were forfeited with the comprehensive reorganisation. Everyone was slightly in fear of Ruscoe and when he took the fifth for algebra nobody slacked. As an outward mark of his status he always wore a mortar board, though partly perhaps to hide his balding head. Apart from other talents he was an excellent cricketer and his presence in matches gave the team a boost.

A friend of Offler's, a clever boy named Davies (the pair excited envious catcalls from the bus boys when they appeared walking side by side sporting the new school straw hats) was the indirect cause of a pleasant social incident when my mother travelled in from Weobley to watch the sports. Since the school lacked a ground of its own the sports were held on Edgar Street field, alongside the cattle market, where, during the winter, Hereford United attracted a crowd of soccer supporters most Saturday afternoons.

My mother and I were seated in the stand when a lady approached and inquired with a smile 'Aren't you Dolly Hambling?' My mother had been called Dolly ever since she was a child, because she was so small. It then appeared that she and Davies's mother had attended the Abergavenny Intermediate School for Girls. As they hadn't met for some thirty years they naturally had much to say. It was a delightful moment during which Davies, who was in the sixth form, while I was in the fourth, and I eyed one another speculatively from a distance. Davies, like his friend, was destined to win an open scholarship to Cambridge, while I followed, much later, to Oxford.

The wearing of straw hats was one of many similar attempts by Ruscoe to upgrade the school. Another was the introduction of rugby football, though he was a soccer man himself. As for the straw hats they made little impact since the majority of boys found them too expensive. Ruscoe's efforts at status-raising proved ultimately successful in as much as the High School subsequently appeared in a history of the public schools as 'a state school in a middle-class area run on public school lines'.

Masters played a major part in our lives but our fellow pupils were just as important. It was the baddies you remember most. Bullying was rife and I suffered my share, since the masters ignored what went on in the playgrounds.

Fatty Jones, a permanently good humoured boy, soon abandoned work for playground football at which he excelled. His weight came in handy when charged by another boy whom he'd bunt out of the way, laughing his head off. When the May Fair came I invited Fatty to join me on the roundabouts and switchbacks. By now the golden Welsh dragons had been superseded by peacocks and whales, but in general things were still much as they had been when we lived in Hereford. There were the traction engines working the dynamos, while the mechanical organs blared forth the latest numbers. Fatty and I had a grand time, though I was amused to discover that he was a trifle nervous as we hurtled up and down inside the big gondolas. Then an odd thing happened. We abandoned the custom of calling one another by nicknames like Fatty or Polly and used instead Kennard and John. Of course as soon as we returned to school our brief friendship ended and we reverted to our customary sobriquets.

During the latter half of my time I palled up with several boys in the upper fifth. Frank Watkins, who came from Woolhope, and Cuthbert Hall from Brockhampton, were farmers' sons. Frank was a delightful laughing extrovert whom I was destined to meet many years later when he was training as a teacher in Devon. Hall played cricket, had a homespun wit and became an accountant. But my best friend was Hubert Wintle, whose father worked for Major Davey at Kinnersley Castle, not far from Weobley. We travelled into school on the same train. Hubert was shy but clever and astonished everyone, except possibly himself, by coming out first in the School Certificate examination. His essential imperturbability acted as a foil to my ebullience and we got on well.

Later I became friendly with Stanley Tute, a new arrival, whose father was vicar of Brilley. Like his father, Stanley was destined for the church. When we all backed Oxford or Cambridge for the boat race he could never make his mind up since his mother was at Cambridge and his father at Oxford.

Weobley still figured prominently in the lives of the High School pupils. The trouble was that we were regarded as village boys who had risen above their normal station, unlike the doctor's sons who attended a Methodist public school and escaped unwelcome attention. We were plagued by the village youths who would yell 'Yah, college boys' and worse. That seemed to be representative of the way the locals felt.

School trips were something of a rarity, at least for train boys who were usually unwilling to make a special journey back to school in order to take part. The only one I remember was travelling with the entire school, including the masters, by train from Hereford to Swindon. Swindon was at that time the town where the engines and rolling stock of the Great Western Railway were made, a circumstance well suited to interest boys. The works were buzzing with activity, with men hammering red-hot steel bars and armies of women busy polishing carriage doors. Most exciting was a new engine undergoing tests. It was mounted on a block of wheels and steamed away furiously while remaining still. Its name, I remember, was *Fawley Court*. In those days the names of certain classes of Great Western engines celebrated the great country houses of the districts through which they passed. There were courts, castles, halls and granges.

Talk of sex was perennial with teenage boys and many delighted in repeating improper tales or limericks. One boy told me, 'We makes 'em up down our way.' To be associated with a girl was to be accredited immediately with every form of vice. In general the sexes were kept separate, even though the Girls' High School was only across the way. Boys met girls from other schools on their way home, some of whom we thought far prettier than the village girls, so we envied them the opportunities denied to us, though what these amounted to was largely fiction. As in the army and the public schools the existence of girls was officially ignored. In fact, few teenagers thought of anything else, their heated imaginations boosted by sheer ignorance.

Nowadays talk (and use) of condoms is so universal that it excites no comment. During the twenties it was far otherwise. One evening the presence of a 'frenchy', as condoms were termed, hanging on the playground railings caused enormous excitement among those who saw it. Its function and contents were described in libidinous terms for those who hadn't.

'They think you don't know nothing about it,' the limerick improvisor remarked concerning his parents' attitude to sex. It was a subject that remained taboo in family life.

During the time we had been living at Weobley new shops had appeared in Hereford, notably a very up-market delicatessen called Fearis in High Town. It was called Ferrises by the boys who bought their lunches there, while others favoured 'Robertses' cafe opposite. Fearis's is ever to be remembered as the place I bought my first slice of veal and ham pie.

We never met any of our village friends in Hereford since travel, even by bus, was expensive. Back at home most were baffled by what I was up to. School had ended for them at fourteen. What in heaven was there to know after that? When I repeated bits of French or quoted an algebraic equation they were duly impressed, though they failed to see its relevance. 'What be the use of it?' they'd ask me and I don't know the answer even now.

19 A Sinking Ship

The year 1929 saw a world recession on a scale which makes recent economic difficulties seem petty. Repercussions were widespread, and our business at Weobley began to decline. At first, we lived in a fool's paradise as my father strove against the odds to increase his trade. He did so minimally by investing in a car so that he could supply remote hamlets off the bus routes, which lacked shops of their own, but it was already too late to save the business. Slowly and inexorably the debts piled up.

At school I had followed the so-called four year course leading to the Cambridge School Certificate. After leaving form IIIB, where I had done well, I went into a steep academic decline. This was partly due to the High School's mathematical and scientific bias, which failed to inspire me. After devoting long periods of the school day wrestling with theorems and equations, we were obliged to spend further hours in the laboratory where we were instructed on how to balance chemical formulae and initiated into the mysteries of heat, light and sound. In all such subjects I failed to excel since they did not then appeal to my imagination. Later in life I took readily to science, but as a schoolboy I was not interested.

Another likely reason for my lack of scholastic success was that I had fallen in love with the minister's daughter. She never knew, and like Dante and Beatrice we never met. I just worshipped from afar.

My father banked with the Midland at Leominster, eight miles from Weobley, and it was my job to cycle over with the payments due on my father's overdraft. I came to know the routine well and often met the manager. I must have made some impression on him because he told my father that he would be prepared to take me on at the bank when I left school. Had this happened my career would have been very different, but fate had other things in store.

Business got worse as the year advanced, and one day the bank manager called on us. It was clear by then that selling up the business could not be long delayed, but life still went on as though nothing had changed.

My interest in birds was an escape route, and wandering by the Brook one day with Jim I found a scrape which had been made by a curlew. Sure enough, when we returned a fortnight later it contained three eggs. I borrowed my father's box camera and photographed instead of stealing them. In fact, I had started to buy eggs through the post. A man named Gowland and another in Somerset supplied lists of eggs at paltry prices, presumably due to the inability of the clientele, mainly schoolboys, to afford much. My collection was

The author's mother and sisters.

continually augmented with rarities from Europe and the Arctic. In those days, the trade in birds' eggs was not controlled by law.

During the spring holidays, Tom and I cycled to Abergavenny. For a change, we took the route through Hay-on-Wye and Talgarth, surprising my aunt and uncle by arriving from an unexpected direction. It was pleasant to stay with people who had no experience of financial disaster and to listen to my uncle reminiscing about his harum-scarum youth. This was the same uncle Dick who had played rugby for Wales and had entertained us with his mouth organ during Christmas 1918. The venue was still the house called Lewes, with its unrivalled prospect across the Usk to the Blorenge.

A WI outing to Cadbury's factory at Bournville helped to take our minds off our growing troubles. We went by bus and the visit was a success. It cost little, and we were served with a fabulous tea of real cream and chocolate cakes, a splendid advertisement for the firm. The Cadbury family were Quakers, like our friends the Manleys, so we would not have expected less.

At last the fateful day arrived when the contents of our house were to be put up for auction. I didn't mind much watching the furniture being heaved onto carts, but it was a wrench to see my mother's piano being pushed away on a trolley by the new farmer at The Ley. Worse was seeing the rocking horse, my sisters' most loved possession, knocked down to a stranger and realising suddenly that I would never see it again. It is a shock to witness family treasures being hauled away as if by robbers and not be able to do anything about it.

George, proprietor of the Red Lion, bought my boxing gloves, not that I missed them. George had always been a good friend, coping with repairing the wireless when the aerial collapsed and replacing the gas lighting with electricity. He was a slight figure with a bushy moustache and everybody liked him. I liked him too, especially when after watching my performance in a school sports he boosted my ego by telling me that I had the makings of a champion high jumper. George had four children, two pretty daughters and two sons. Jim, our help, had long loved the elder girl while half the boys in school were keen on Maisie with her long beribboned plaits. The elder son soon passed from view learning to be a farmer, but the younger boy and his father failed to see eye to eye. When George lost his temper they would engage in a chase, and it was amusing to see them rushing around the garden, George shouting threats. We were not the only ones to leave Weobley in those hard times. George and his family soon followed.

It was a boon to be able to keep our books. They included big reference works like *The Treasure House* and *Harmsworth's Encyclopaedia*; both sets of volumes I still study and read. My father did me a great service by buying books when he could afford it.

The Taits bought the shop for a song, but I don't know what happened to the Ford. Probably they bought it to sell, as they were in the car business. When all was over we went to the Manleys for tea. For the first time in my life I had no home to go to. The Manleys could not have known, as they waved us goodbye, that they would soon be following in our wake when the owners of their property foreclosed.

We were collected by my aunt Ethel in her car, but had got only to the top of Steam Mill Bank when my mother remembered that she had forgotten something. It fell to me to run back to Manleys, an awful anticlimax in the circumstances. Mrs. Manley was still in the sitting room when I arrived and quickly found the missing article. As I ran back up the street for what was to be the last time I heard behind me a blackbird carolling, only it wasn't a blackbird. It was our whistler Ernie Hill.

That was my farewell to Weobley, and the memory has remained with me down the years.

20 Exit and Return

Just before we left Weobley I cycled down to the brook and carved my name on the bridge. It was an instinctive parting gesture. The July evening was fine, with the Black Mountains etched against the western sky. I wondered whether I would ever see them again, or Jim or Johnny, not to mention my blonde goddess the minister's daughter who was constantly in my thoughts. 'I expect there'll be a pike lying there', my father had remarked the first time we saw the Brook some seven years previously. It was then February fill-dyke and my father was trying to compensate for the loss of the Wye. But there was no pike, or indeed any fish at all, though we did not know it then.

Now that we had left Weobley, the question was: what did the future hold? I was fifteen, no great age, but still a year older than my contemporaries who had remained at the village school, most of whom were now employed locally. I had been shipwrecked, as it were, in midstream and the way ahead was uncertain. The papers spoke of two million unemployed and rising, and a feeling of instability was gripping the western world. A dictator had appeared in Italy and there was growing political unrest throughout Europe. 'You ought to enter a sixth form', Ashton, my form master, had advised when he heard that I was leaving. That would have meant a further two or even three years at school when I should have been earning a living.

In the meantime we settled in Exeter but were not forgotten by Weobley people. Miss Annie Hall was among the first visitors, followed by Miss Manley. Then one day Mrs. Norman arrived, accompanied by her young son. She told us all the gossip and brought us up to date with what was going on in Herefordshire. Little had changed, it seemed, though the bakery in the centre of the village had suffered a disastrous fire. Philip and Ellen Foster came to talk over old times, as did the doctor's son, who had been friendly with my father. It was good to know that we weren't forgotten and to hear about old acquaintances and the children I had grown up with.

All my life I had hoped to go to Oxford, and rode about on Boat Race day wearing a dark blue rosette, but entrance to Oxford was destined to be delayed. After further schooling I lowered my sights and graduated from the local university college. After a period at Exeter School learning to be a teacher, and a short spell at Sherborne, I eventually secured a post at Herne Bay College. I was commissioned into the Officer's Training Corps, and when war broke out was able to transfer to the Devonshire Regiment and later to the King's African Rifles. When I was demobbed I decided to visit Hereford as the demob centre was not far away. I had been away for sixteen years but found the

High School much the same. Even the staff had changed little apart from the death of the art and geography master Pym Wilson. Little Wattie had retired and one or two new masters had been appointed. Only Ruscoe, the headmaster, remembered me as the boy who rarely did himself justice in examinations. Witts was pleased to learn that I probably owed my interview at Herne Bay College to him since he had been friendly with the headmaster at Oxford.

Ashton walked back with me. When we reached High Town I drew his attention to Lloyds Bank and told him that I had once lived on those premises. He did not remember Walmsley's, which had been converted many years earlier.

Plenty of familiar shops remained including Greenland's, Boots, and Ralph & Clark's. The old Penny Bazaar had become Marks & Spencer during my time at the High School, but now, like its neighbour Woolworth's, it appeared bigger than ever. At the entrance to Church Street I found Jones's still functioning as a sweet shop although the name had changed. I remembered Jones, a big man with a florid face, but now there was somebody new.

The Castle Green was my next port of call and I was delighted to find it looking the same. The old cannon on which we used to climb had gone, as had the drinking tap, but that was all. Even the pebble beach survived, where my father and I had fished almost a quarter of a century previously. The Victoria Bridge remained intact, but a new road bridge had been built a short distance upstream from the old one to cope with the increasing traffic. First impressions last longest and mine were still centred on this area within easy reach of the city centre, where I had played as a child and roamed as a schoolboy.

By the time I returned some years later on my honeymoon I had been to Oxford at last, lectured at St Andrews and Bangor, and started to write a series of adventure and travel books, mainly about Africa, as well as more serious volumes. The city had by now been opened up with broad new thoroughfares. Aylestone Hill, up which Nana had pushed the pram, was now busy and dangerous. I took my wife to see Castle Green, still as it was, before going on to Weobley.

My first impression was that nothing had happened since I left. The shop was still there, converted into a garage and run by none other than the fiddler's younger brother Gardner Tait. In the Red Lion we caught up with the news, but that was precious little. Business was slow, Gardner said, and he was rarely asked for more than a single gallon of petrol. One major change was the conversion of the Gobbutts, the former cricket ground, into a housing estate of imposing villas. Many of the black and white village houses were now the homes of commuters and retired people. There was a new secondary school near Pepperplock.

Gardener Tait and the author.

The old school in Broad Street had been turned into a shop, but what was most surprising Garnstone Castle was no more. It had presumably been found uneconomic to run it, so it had been demolished to the last stone. Another landmark, the Park Meadow, had been drained and reverted to growing hay. The Bearcroft pool had also been drained, so there was no more sliding and skating there in winter. Even the Nap had disappeared and been lost in the surrounding meadow, while the Workhouse had been converted into flats.

By happy chance my wife and I found ourselves in Hereford during May Fair week. I had forgotten the significance of the date until we started to drive into town, only to find the roads closed to traffic as in years gone by. We parked and walked in, and memories flooded back. There were stalls along Broad Street in front of the Green Dragon, as there had been in the nineteen twenties, only I saw no coconut shies or skittles. I noticed the absence of the magnificent showmen's traction engines with their great yellow wheels and tall chimneys, but the spirit of the fair was alive and strong as we discovered later in the evening. Meanwhile, we strolled down to the Castle Green, pausing to admire the swans on the pool and the fine shrubberies and tiered rustic seats.

The author and his old school at Weobley.

Later, back at the fair, we watched the crowd assembling outside Lloyds Bank, just as an earlier generation had done when Lloyds was still Walmsley's. There were no golden dragons for them to ride, but faster and more ingenious machines. By comparison with the May Fairs I recalled it all seemed efficient and streamlined, but less ornate and earthy. Alas, there were no fair organs.

In an era of change, tradition makes for stability. I was delighted to discover that the old May Fair hadn't been banished to a field outside the city. Many places keep their fairs by right of ancient charter, and May is a popular month – the winter has gone, summer is coming and it is time to look forward, perhaps to something important like a change of job or simply to a couple of evenings of bright lights, noise and fun. It is the time to cock a snook at solemnity and – in my time literally – to let your hair down. I finish where I began, with the roar of the May Fair around me.

Hereford and Herefordshire: I went away long ago, but each return visit brings a deep nostalgia. My childhood home was here, and the ghosts remain.